July '04

Susan,

Thank you for the
opportunity to work
together.

All my best,

Additional Praise for *Choose What Works*

"The future of business lies with the people who can envision compelling opportunities and lead others to fulfill those dreams. Howard Goldman has given us a proven *five-star* recipe for success. Roll up your sleeves and start cookin'!"

—Peter Hirshberg, CEO, *Gloss.com*

"I have known Howard Goldman for 20 years as friend, colleague, and *performance coach*. He and his powerful *System*™ are always there to support my leadership, my vital relationship to people—and the results which are at the core of being the GM of a multinational division, or CEO of a high-tech start-up."

**—Keith Schaefer (Fmr.) GM, *NEC Technologies*;
CEO, *Liquid Thinking***

"In *Choose What Works,* Howard Goldman shares the essence of 25 years of work with top performing executives globally. He offers us a fresh, compelling, and accessible guide to transform our work life and our valued relationships."

—Kimberly Jenkins, Ph.D. Founder, *Highway One*

"Howard Goldman helped me crack some of the toughest organizational problems I'd ever confronted. Now you can harness the power of his proprietary *System*™. Get ready for a totally new way of thinking about, acting on—and ultimately achieving results."

**—Rex Golding (Fmr.) Managing Director,
*Morgan Stanley Technology Banking Group***

"These simple, yet thought-provoking insights on *Choose What Works* have yielded dramatic results for my business—our profits tripled. Goldman's *Operating System*™ is the new basis of how I make decisions and have life work."

—Zen Ohashi, Founder, *Management Coach Network*, Tokyo, Japan

"*Choose What Works* contains as much wisdom as any book I know. You are holding a valuable tool in your hand; make something happen with it."

—Gene Golub, Chairman, *Golub & Co.*

CHOOSE WHAT WORKS

The Proven Secrets *to* Professional Greatness

HOWARD GOLDMAN

AMERICA'S TOP PERFORMANCE COACH

WYNNEFIELD BUSINESS PRESS

SAN CARLOS, CA

Published by:
Wynnefield Business Press
770 Crestview Dr.
San Carlos, CA 94070
WynnefieldBusinessPress.com

Publisher's Cataloguing-in-Publication Data
Goldman, Howard
    Choose what works : the proven secrets to professional greatness / Howard
    Goldman. –San Carlos, CA : Wynnefield Business Press, 2003.

        p. ; cm
        ISBN: 0-9729643-0-4

    1. Success in business. 2. Success. 3. Self-realization. I. Title.

HF5386 .G65 2003   2003104088
650.1–dc21   0308

Project coordination by Jenkins Group • www. bookpublishing.com
Cover design and interior illustrations by Dale Hortsman
Interior layout by Debbie Sidman/Paw Print Media
Cover photos by Kristen Loken

Printed in the United States of America

07 06 05 04 03 • 5 4 3 2 1

In Memory

James Sachs

1955–2002

Jim's life is a model for the achievement
and heart that is embodied in this book.

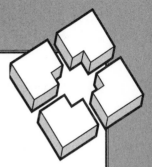

User's guide

Acknowledgments

---◆·◆---

"A real book is not one that we read, but one that reads us."
—W. H. AUDEN, POET

---◆·◆---

This book is dedicated to Lisa Miller Goldman, my wife and partner. Her encouragement was the moving force in bringing this book to fruition. She fills my sails with her faith in me and animates my heart with love and appreciation. She is the best consultant I know.

My measure of success for this publication is, in part, that my children Hazi and Rose will be able to pick this book off the shelf in ten years and be proud of its relevance and meaning to them.

I am grateful to all my clients and colleagues who have contributed to my work and career and formed the basis for the insights and practices I present in this book. My laboratory is observing their courage, fortitude, and skill in the face of the challenges they accept and meet daily.

I am especially indebted (in alphabetical order) to Ann Acierno, Paul Adams, Roy Agostino, Jeri Allen, Paul Allen, Sueann Ambron, David Archambault, Frank Armstrong, Greg Ballard, Ted Barnett, Jim Bartlett, Elise Bauer, Scott Beechuk, Fritz Beesemyer, Larry Bein, Mike Bell, Ken Bero, Kathryn Besemer, Elias Blowie, Martha Borst, Claire Buchanan, Gervase Bushe, Brian Cannon, Bob Cheatham, Bob Clemens, Jack Clewis, Bud Colligan, Burt Cummings, Elaine Cummings, Kirk Cunningham, Alan Curtis, Peter de Verteuil, John Demsey, Bob Downs, Kevin Elias,

Tony Espinoza, Bob Faber, Bruce Falck, Scott Fey, Kendall Fitzhugh, Vangie Flandez, Ed Forman, Phil Foster, John Fraissinet, Jon Gans, Peter George, Bill Gibson, Bernie Gifford, Tony Gilroy, Alex Godelman, Rex Golding, Kathryn Goldman, Gene Golub, Mark Greenfield, Jim Gregg, Jill Griffen, Mike Gullard, Marcelo Gumucio, Martin Haeberli, Guy Hains, Ed Hartford, Kevin Hartz, Randy Haykin, Christie Hefner, Paul Herschberger, Peter Hirshberg, Wes Hoffman, John Holland, Brendon Hughes, Carla Ison, John Ison, Bill Jacobs, Carol Jacobsen, Jason Jay, Kimberly Jenkins, James Joaquin, Tom Johnson, Ed Jordan, Peter Katz, Tom Kilcoyne, Anita Kopec, Richard Kreitman, Claudia L'Amoreaux, Gary Lauder, William Lauder, Lee Boon Huat, Ellen Levy, Ivor Lewis, Jeff Locke, Dana Lyon, Lloyd Mahaffey, Miles Mahoney, Teri Malloy, Gary Marcotte, Robert Marick, Doug Marquis, Tom Martin, Dennis McEniry, Tim McLaughlin, Ivy Millman, Roger Morgan, Gary Morris, Wyatt Mullin, Page Murray, Mike Newman, Carl Nichols, Gunnar Nilsson, Aleksey Novicov, Zen Ohashi, Ann O'Malley, Betsy Pace, Van Pell, Tom Pomeroy, Andrew Preston, Kate Purmal, Andy Raskin, John Rivlin, Antonio Rizzo, Heidi Roizen, Javier Rojas, Kristee Rosendahl, Steve Russell, Ann Sachs, Chris Sachs, Keith Schaefer, Kathy Schlein, Steve Schlemmer, Bob Sick, Steve Silverman, Bob Smith, Ted Tannenbaum, Bill Tobin, Phil Vachon, Rick Van Hoesen, Pam Van Zandt, Barry Waitte, Greg Wolfe, Liz Wilkerson, Ken Wirt, Edward Wong, Janet Wood, Gail Yoshimoto.

To my coaches, mentors, and fellow pioneers in the body of work that gave rise to my development: Reuben and Ethel Goldman, Sydney and Carl Tinkelman, Sy and Fran Miller, Jack and Carol Weber, Charles Smith, Jim Selman, Tom Drucker, Mike Nichols, Lynn Gorodsky, Sondra Card, Michael and Arlene Reid, Mike MacMaster, David Spiwack, Anne Adams, Jack Rosenberg, Deepak Chopra, and Fernando Flores.

My editors, Laurie Rozakis, Sue McManus, and Devon Ritter, using different methods, each contributed a great deal. I am most grateful for their assistance and work on this project. Although they were sometimes tough "graders," the final product was enhanced in many ways by virtue of their diligence and skill. Additionally, Dale Horstman's fine design, and all the folks at the Jenkins Group—Jerry, Nikki, Kim, Kelli, and Leah, added to the quality and reach of this project.

Thank you to all my family and friends, who complete my community of relationships. Please forgive me if I haven't cited you directly.

And to my team members Mystic and Quik, whose lessons of loyalty, patience, and unqualified love are constant gifts.

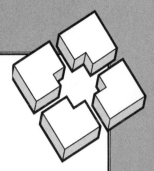

Preface

I have written this book for you.

You're probably similar in many ways to my clients: intelligent, accomplished people who are interested in greater levels of success and professional satisfaction. The more open to learning and self-discovery and the hungrier for accomplishment you are, the more value you will receive from what I have to offer.

I've written *Choose What Works* to share with you the benefits of my experience contributing to the lives and careers of people I've worked with at client companies. The creation of this book represents the distillation of a proprietary set of processes I have developed over twenty-five years in my career as an international management consultant and performance coach. It is about applying an alternative yet accessible system to the way we conventionally approach achievement. I call this alternate way of thinking, planning, and taking action to accelerate accomplishment and satisfaction the *High-Performance Operating System*™.

Choose What Works will guide your achievements at work and in life. It will lead you through practical steps to fulfill your ambitions. It will also provide you with a useful perspective on how to overcome default modes of thought and self-limiting practices.

Before we begin to work with and appreciate the usefulness of this system, let me give you a better sense of who I am and how I came to be a consultant and performance coach to outstanding people around the world.

The origins of my work

My career has always been guided by bridging the unlikely bedfellows of commerce and art. In college, I realized that the only way I was going to make it through the educational system was to study something I was passionate about (this was the '60s, man!), so I built a degree around my interests in film directing, advertising, and mass media. The day I graduated, despite the loving consternation of my family, I took the freeway 2,700 miles to Hollywood to realize my dreams.

I subsisted on oatmeal and coffee while struggling to break into the seemingly unassailable fortress of the Hollywood establishment. One day, I applied to an anonymous ad in the *LA Times* that vaguely described a job in the "record business." The job, I subsequently learned, was at Capitol Records/EMI. Capitol was undergoing serious commercial challenges in being able to market credibly to the changing tastes of the "youth market" and was doing a national search for someone to help them do this. Out of the 200 applicants, I landed the job and found myself working as a wide-eyed marketing project manager. My foot was in the door.

At Capitol, I functioned in a unique capacity. I had access to senior management, recording artists, and their handlers, and an ear to the trends that were unfolding on the "street." Given the befuddlement of some of the senior executives in the business, I exhibited a refreshing confidence. In a sea of hesitancy, I was willing to say, "I know." I was willing to speak my mind, express my enthusiasms, identify bullshit when I saw it, and step wholeheartedly into the opportunities to act and to demonstrate my skills: discernment, intuition, self-expression, and an innate sense of what would emerge as a viable commercial success.

My friends from school declared I had "the best job in America." I moved up the ladder and became the Director of Artist Development for Capitol Records/EMI. My job was to identify and promote a myriad of success stories: the Beatles, Pink Floyd, Leon Russell, The Band, Merle Haggard, Linda Rondstadt. I developed an ongoing parade of various other performing artists, as well. Some succeeded; some didn't. "What causes success?" I asked myself constantly. The question became a mantra for me as I searched for a ready formula. The pursuit of the answer was like peeling the skin of an onion; each layer revealed unsatisfactory answers and deeper questions.

I was a Rock Star in my own mind, yet a disturbing thought was tugging at the hem of my paisley bellbottoms—the music business, as I plied it, was somehow desperate, shallow, and undignified. As I worshipped at the exalted altar of pop culture, I kept wondering, "Is this all there is?" This question along with my desire to understand the nature of success served as navigational points in my professional and personal journey.

Changes

In 1973, I was ready for another challenge, so I left Hollywood and moved to the greener pastures of northern California. I thought I had put together enough money in the fast lane to retire to my version of the contemplative life of a country gentleman. The mantra "What causes success?" accompanied me as a persistent guide. I traveled widely. I pursued graduate studies in psychology, business, and linguistics. I studied with spiritual masters and contemporary teachers in the Bay Area of San Francisco. I immersed myself in the emerging cultural stream of personal transformation.

The realities of earning a living, supporting young children, and establishing a viable new profession thrust me back into the world of commerce. I started a business as an executive recruiter, in the electric environment of Silicon Valley, just south of San Francisco. My work was now to find executive talent for demanding, fast-growth, high-tech companies. Over the next three years, I built the company to employ 27 professionals in three divisions.

The epicenter of the Digital Age, Silicon Valley attracted the best and the brightest from around the globe. I found that my interest was sharing with clients and employees what I had learned in pursuing my question: "What causes success?" My enthusiasm for contributing what I knew was expressed effortlessly, and I delivered practical job-related insights with passion. I wanted my clients to benefit from my coaching by having an advantage over the competition when they interviewed for a job. Most did.

I stayed in touch with many of the professionals I had placed. They told me of the challenges and issues they faced in coming up to speed in their new positions. I began to offer ideas for more efficient management and methods for improved communications. A new opportunity emerged as I assisted former job candidates to structure their leadership agenda and build important relationships with their staff. I offered an attentive ear to the difficulties they shouldered in learning to be a manager in a rapidly changing company culture. I suggested perspectives they could consider and described ways for them to communicate clearly and act boldly. My role was gratifying as I witnessed my clients' increased effectiveness.

Soon, more of my clients were calling and asking: "Remember what we talked about? Could you spend some time with my staff and give them the benefit of your approach?" An exciting yet not wholly formed opening developed. The opportunity that dawned on me was to professionally apply everything I'd learned while pursuing the question "What causes success?" to an emerging career direction. Knowing that everything begins with a first courageous step, I opened the consulting division of my firm, Management Associates, in 1978.

From that early professional interest in capturing and sharing the formulas for success, over the past quarter-century as a coach and consultant I have pursued a career of study, experimentation, and engagement with thousands of people, individually and in teams. I've been dedicated to the development of high performance in a broad array of industries and distinguished companies in North America, Europe, and Japan. My clients have included Apple computer, AOL Time Warner, NEC, Land Rover, Morgan Stanley, Disney, and Estée Lauder, as well as scores of high-tech start-ups.

As my work evolved, it gathered and included the influences and terminology of the industries in which I applied it. Entertainment and technology flowed into common avenues of content. Human factors and applications of computer know-how were woven together in our experience and imagination. Performance, networks, communication—the metaphors of the Digital Age came together at work, at home, and in the laboratory of my inquiry with clients and colleagues. We were building powerful new tools and systems to help people create their future. The image of a *High-Performance Operating System*, as we will discover, became a natural carrier for transmission of this viable work to others.

During this remarkable ride, I have been a student, manager, partner, marketer, husband, father, teacher, university lecturer, venture investor, consultant, business founder, professional coach, and a coach of coaches. My greatest lessons that prepared me for coaching have come in the course of my work as an entrepreneur in a series of ventures. It is there that I learned to stand in the fire.

About this book

This book is the result of observing what works—and what doesn't. My successes—and as important, my setbacks—aided me in developing the compassion to offer the insights and tools that will support you in achieving your aspirations.

> "Winning isn't everything. Wanting to is."
>
> —CATFISH HUNTER, BASEBALL PLAYER

Far beyond raising your interest and entertaining your curiosity, *Choose What Works* will give you the opportunity to develop a new and empowering relationship with yourself, your world, and others. I promise to guide you through a working blueprint to reach the levels of success and personal satisfaction that you seek and are willing to attain.

I wrote this book for you. Make the most of the opportunity.

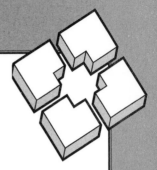

Introduction

This book is conceived as a vehicle to support your achievements. I have created an effective toolkit for you to use in your work and in other areas of your life where you seek greater accomplishment. Most people apply the coaching to work, so most of the examples and exercises are directed at this arena. However, you will find that the personal aspects of communication and relationship usually come into play as they underpin your primary professional ambitions.

The foundation of this work is a set of compelling ideas and questions. These concepts are designed to guide you to view your work, your life, and your current practices in an alternative light. You will then be free to make choices that are consistent with your freely chosen intentions rather than shaped by your history.

I will challenge you at times with views and perceptions that cause you to pause, to make new connections to your life and career, and to ask, "What is my authentic response?" I invite you to press forward and strengthen your ability to understand new concepts and forge different interpretations. Something is often lost or diminished when every detail is explained. Stay with questions that go beyond the obvious, such as "How do I know that to be true?"

In some cases, I will structure your progression through the development of your plans and actions so that you think creatively and courageously. I will encourage you to discuss questions such as "What does he mean by that?" with your friends and associates. Bridging the gaps with your own questions, your experiences, and your imaginative acts is enriching.

Your road map

The design of *Choose What Works* is not arbitrary. I developed the process that we'll use with the participation of thousands of people in companies, large and small, around the globe. Given an opportunity to separate themselves from the gravitational pull of reactive thinking and deadening corporate rituals, these individuals moved to exceptional heights. With the benefit of a structured approach, people working together to produce significant results advance surprisingly similar patterns of dialogue and invention.

> "In the absence of coherent, systematic design, you can't distinguish activity from progress."
> —NEWT GINGRICH, POLITICIAN AND ACADEMIC

Working with these groups, I developed a number of essential steps, which were refined as we tested and the evolved the process—here are some examples proven to be most rewarding as we worked together:

1. Guiding participants to set initial expectations that they would most value in completing the process.
2. Making sense out of the past and registering concerns without becoming captive to historic fears and previously unsuccessful plans.
3. Proceeding along a set of structured discussions that promote creative thinking among attendees and ultimately

result in forming commitments that are endorsed and coordinated within the group.

4. Conceiving a collective intent that has relevance and importance and is agreed upon in a remarkably short time through an ordered approach.

5. Developing credible objectives that anchor uniform yet rigorous planning activities. These plans are the product of collaboration and multiple inputs.

6. Identifying barriers to success for groups and individuals and systematically working to overcome or remove them.

7. Resolving emerging problems at the heart of daily operations through effective practices of communication, innovation, and synchronizing.

8. Making meaningful connections to the objectives they have crafted, and to each other, participants are able to specify their role and shape the specific contribution required by others.

9. Implementing reliable methods for ongoing planning, management, and review.

10. Acknowledging and honoring participation by all members, to encourage continued contribution to and satisfaction in the process.

I have written *Choose What Works* to make these reliable approaches available to you as you read and work through the book. Specifically, I have compiled each stage of progress into a "road map," or framework of planning and action. This road map corresponds to each chapter in the book for this journey you are about to embark on.

Road map of *Choose What Works*

1.0 **Your specs for success**
Setting expectations and defining systems

2.0 **Words make worlds**
Accounting for the past

Your success will be based on responsibly applying this framework of planning and action, which unfolds in the following chapters, to your current situation and aspirations. Your role is to express yourself fully and completely. You will gain confidence and build momentum as you start to work with material that is vital to you. As you move comfortably through the steps I have outlined in the road map, you will be guided in the design and development of your unique plan.

As you progress through each chapter, you will have the opportunity to adapt the format of the book to your specific interests. Each chapter develops the framework for planning and improving your direction. You'll use the outcomes you specify in navigating through the book. Along the way, you'll incorporate new points of view, build a richer field of details that clarify and strengthen your focus, and become increasingly skillful at communicating with precision.

Going forward, we'll account for where you've been, where you are now, and where you choose to go.

I have designed each chapter of *Choose What Works* to reflect common elements that will provide continuity and deepen your experience:

- *Previews* begin each chapter and outline the subsections that follow.
- *Displays* illustrate key points though graphics and text.
- *Spec Sheets* are constructed for you to write your responses to specific questions and develop your plans. Examples of sample responses are provided when useful.
- *Store in Memory* are highlights found at the conclusion of each chapter and summarize the key learning points.
- *Cornerstones of the High-Performance Operating System* are inserted at four appropriate stages of your progress in the text. They are displayed as a full set just prior to Chapter 1.0.

I have often used *italics* to call attention to terms of reference and metaphors that are related to the High-Performance Operating System. Many of these expressions are highlighted in the Glossary at the back of this book.

Other proprietary elements of the High-Performance Operating System, such as your Focused Intent™, Pathways for Action™, and Problem Resolution Methodology™, are represented in capitals to highlight their structure within the overall framework of this book and the technology of accomplishment that it represents.

"Your life is the sum result of all the choices you make, both consciously and unconsciously. If you can control the process of choosing, you can take control of all aspects of your life. You can find the freedom that comes from being in charge of yourself."

—Robert F. Bennett, U.S. Senator

Keep your eye on ...

You will trace your movement onward, in part, by resolving issues and concerns and removing barriers to your goals. You and I will employ powerful tools to move you reliably through any roadblocks you encounter while you establish new networks of support.

As you move forward, we'll look for ways to track progress and value accomplishments. Each step will build on the shoulders of previous work and leave you more able to measure and appreciate what you've achieved. You'll then be ready to take on the next challenge.

You can proceed at your own pace with the work. Most readers initially cover the entire process in about a week. However, I encourage you to then schedule progress reviews at 30-day intervals after your initial plan and first steps in enacting what you've envisioned. These periodic reviews will assist you in extending your understanding of my system and adjust your actions for implementation.

At the outset, you'll most likely read *Choose What Works* on your own. You will, of course, increase the impact of your personal achievement plan by involving others in the early stages of your thinking as soon as you are comfortable. In Chapter 9.0, "Network Protocols," though, I will ask you to formally develop relationships with others who can understand your intentions, collaborate to improve your planning, and support the progress of your actions. Working with a partner or coach, or bringing this process to a group, will unquestionably multiply your effectiveness and sharpen your focus.

A *visionary* is someone who sees what's missing first and acts to provide it.

The essence of this book is for you to accrue the benefits of working with a world-class performance coach. The rules that govern coaching relationships are covered in depth in Chapter 10, "There Shall Be Coaching." To maximize the value of our relationship now, follow the instructions that shape each chapter.

In my role as a performance coach and consultant, I constantly remind myself of seven key ideas that help me lead workshops on the ideas we will cover in *Choose What Works*. I offer the following guidelines to boost your effectiveness.

Guidelines for effectiveness

1. Enjoy yourself, and have fun with people and new ideas.
2. Go for it, especially when you may feel more secure staying with known habits and comfortable routines.
3. Stay connected to others while pressing forward with the agenda.
4. Risk looking foolish. It is a small price you pay to express yourself fully.
5. Communicate honestly and courageously.
6. Trust yourself, trust the process, and trust the power of committed people you invite to join you in *Choose What Works*.
7. A *visionary* is someone who sees what's missing first and acts to provide it.

Four cornerstones of your High-Performance Operating System

 ## Cornerstone 1

When people create something, they tend to own, protect, nurture, sustain, and fulfill it.

 ## Cornerstone 2

Envision a possibility and commit to its fulfillment before you necessarily have the experience, resources, or know-how to achieve it.

 ## Cornerstone 3

Systematically identify and resolve barriers that are inconsistent with your intended results.

 ## Cornerstone 4

High performance occurs in a medium of communication and relationship.

CHAPTER 1.0

Your Specs for Success
Setting expectations and defining systems

"Working successfully is a participation sport."

—Silicon Valley venture capitalist

 Preview

1.1 Your operating system Your operating system underlies everything you do. Given this bold statement and the significance of understanding the notion of an operating system as the foundation of improved performance, I'll define what we're referring to and why it matters so you can develop your choices in *Choose What Works*.

1.2 Your expectations Somewhere in the mix of your instincts that attracted you to this book is the potential to move forward, to go beyond what you've been settling for, to restore your confidence and passion for new challenges. Your articulation of these expectations will become the foundation on which to build a new future.

1.3 Set the cornerstones The first of four cornerstones that define the High-Performance Operating System that we will be developing and applying toward your success.

1.1   Your *operating system*

Your *operating system* underlies everything you do. Given this bold statement and the significance of understanding the notion of an operating system as the foundation of improved performance, let's define what we're referring to and why it matters.

Your *operating system* underlies everything you do.

To begin, a disclaimer: I am not a "techie." However, it is hard to imagine a business or area of personal communication that hasn't been fundamentally changed by the advent of computer technology and its myriad applications. You are most likely not an engineer, and your interest is in improving your performance and satisfaction. So what's the importance of the operating system metaphor? And what does it have to do with your ability to perform?

In my work with executive teams over the years, one challenge I've faced is succinctly presenting the underlying "motivational" processes that govern performance and accomplishment. When I apply the metaphor of a computer operating system to human thought and action, I strike an immediate chord. Clients quickly connect abstract concepts such as awareness and motivation to the more graphic elements of digital technology: systems, networks, and instruction sets.

Computer scientists with whom I work commonly define an operating system as:

> "The main control program that schedules tasks, manages storage, and handles communication. Its core part is always present, and all applications must communicate with the operating system."

Keeping the above definition in mind, read the following characteristics as if you were describing the internal process of a human being:

- We are examining how a system (like a computer; like you and me) communicates (talks) to itself and its constituent parts.
- An operating system provides a platform of instruction on top of which other programs, called *applications*, can run.
- Your choice of operating system determines to a great extent the applications, or tasks, that can be performed.
- As a user, you normally interact with the operating system through a set of commands.
- The operating system is for the most part transparent, that is, invisible to us as users.

In summary the operating system is designed to drive performance, connect with resources, support the achievement of tasks, and satisfy users.

Display 1.1 (see next page) illustrates the parallels between a computer operating system and our human process.

Our human "operating system" is composed of thoughts, emotions, and reactions. These thoughts, emotions, and reactions are a form of communication that is sent and received in a silent "conversation" we conduct in our head. This internal conversation is mostly unobserved moment by moment.

As with the computer, the human *operating system* can be understood as the main control program, or *platform*, that is always present. This unexamined operating layer drives (or conversely limits) our performance, our achievement, our ability to connect to others, and our sense of ourselves.

One further parallel, for now: the operating system in our computer is written and runs in computer code, or *language*. As the computer performs various tasks, it translates high-level *commands* into basic code that it can *execute*. In the core of every computer system, primary language is composed entirely of 1s and 0s. I will refer to human's primary language also as I expand on the nature and performance of our systems of thought, emotion, and reaction.

Display 1.1 *Operating Systems—*computer and human

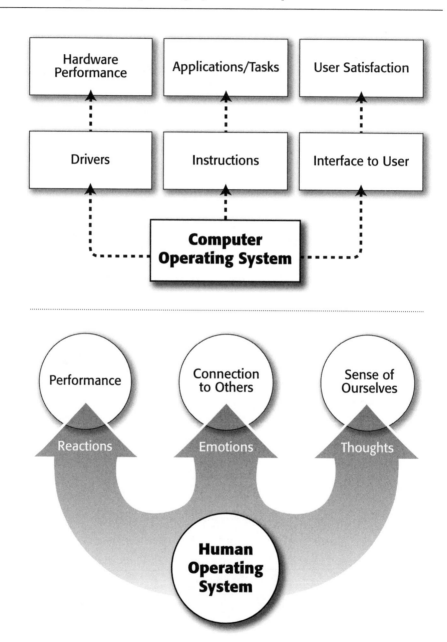

In our human operating system, consider that all experience—images, senses, memories, desires, reactions, and feelings—is ultimately revealed to us in language. Yes, some of us feel things directly or see in vivid images of color or emotional tone. I find it interesting that if you ask some people "How do you know you dream in color?" they will describe in *words* what they experience. If you ask others "How are you feeling?" they will, perhaps with some effort, *tell* you about hurt, joy, or pleasure. At our core, our relationships with each other, with ourselves, and ultimately with life are given meaning through language.

> "We human beings belong to language. In language we love and hate, we admire and despise. We interpret our crises as individual and social. We suffer, and exalt, and despair. In language, we receive the gift of being human. All the feeling, the thinking, the action, and the things of the world as we know it are given to us in language."
>
> —FERNANDO FLORES, PHILOSOPHER AND ENTREPRENEUR

As Helen Keller, rendered deaf and blind by a childhood bout of meningitis, said when she learned her first words, the entire world became possible. "When I learned the meaning of 'I' and 'me' and found that I was something, I began to think. Then consciousness first existed for me."[1]

I will return to a deeper understanding of your operating system, and how you can gain new access to its modes of performance, as *Choose What Works* unfolds. For now, I ask you to look at your expectations in reading and working through this book. Your expectations will serve as a foundation on which to install a system that will produce new standards of operation.

1.2   Your expectations

You've begun reading *Choose What Works* for a reason. What is it? Maybe you're curious about what's offered on the cover or about learning more about my approach to increased achievement. It's likely that you're seeking greater satisfaction in your career and more effective communication with others. What's going on at work? What's

---

[1]Helen Keller, *The Story of My Life*, (New York: Doubleday, Page and Co., 1905, p. 51)

happening in your relationships? What's occurring in your life for which *Choose What Works* will be a solution?

Somewhere in the mix of your instincts that attracted you to this book is the potential to move forward, to go beyond what you've been settling for, to restore your confidence and passion for new challenges. I encourage you to read this book with an interest in thoroughly and deeply examining aspects of your work and life.

A key part of the experience of *Choose What Works* is participating fully by completing the processes and exercises that I've designed. By engaging 100 percent with these elements of the book, you will be able to translate the benefits of performance coaching to achieve what you intend. Initially, the value will come from your thoughtful written responses to the exercises developed on the *Spec Sheets*, which I've included to accompany each of your steps forward.

The first *Spec Sheet*, which looks at your expectations of the results of working with this book, will give a baseline measure of where and how you are entering the process.

Spec Sheet 1.2: "Your expectations" is an opportunity to take a snapshot of your current views in significant areas of your work and life. This is also where you can initially determine the level of progress that would satisfy you in working with the tools I am providing. At the end of the book, we'll check back to the expectations you've written to assess what you've gained, what's actively in progress, and what's next.

"Don't chew on the menu thinking you are eating the meal."

In a moment, I'll ask you to take a major step forward by writing in the space provided on the subsequent pages. First a note of caution.

As one of my mentors pointed out to me when I was intellectualizing the action from the sidelines, "Don't chew on the menu thinking you are eating the meal." When I realized what she was saying about the requirement to participate fully, I was able to catch myself more often as I unconsciously traded direct experience for overanalyzing and judging from the sidelines. I often fooled myself by thinking I was in the game when I was merely on the bench.

This book will have the most impact when you think fully and creatively and then respond genuinely in writing where requested. Trust me on this: clarifying your thoughts in written form is powerful. New levels of clarity and unexpected resolve result from the simple act of getting stuff out of your head and onto paper. The process of distilling your thoughts in written form subtly shifts how you regard situations and alternatives. Nobody's watching; however, the opportunity here is to gain everything that you came for.

Now it's time to write your expectations on *Spec Sheet 1.2.*

 ## SPEC SHEET 1.2—YOUR EXPECTATIONS

Complete the following questions with your authentic views and expectations. (Example responses are provided.)

After reading *Choose What Works*, I expect …

in my effectiveness at work, to be able to:

(Organize, plan, and lead my staff better)
_____

_____

_____

to produce results at work, such as: (name areas of desired results)

(Be promoted to a director of marketing)
_____

_____

_____

others will see me as:

(A strong leader and good communicator)
_____

_____

in my satisfaction in my career to:

(Accelerate my advance to VP Marketing)

_____

_____

to be able to communicate effectively with: (name persons)

(John, boss; and my staff, especially Nancy)

_____

_____

so they realize that:

(I am competent and able to lead effectively)

_____

_____

in the area of my relationships, to feel:

(More connection with others and better understood)

_____

_____

to fulfill my dreams in new areas of life, such as:

(Eventually start my own marketing business)

_____

_____

1.3   Set the cornerstones

You and I have the gift of creation. The power to create comes from our words, our language, and our visions. When we originate something—an idea, a project, a new future—we experience a potent relationship to what we have formed. We feel pride of ownership. We understand the situation and the challenge that gave rise to our creation, and we recognize the new possibilities that it represents. We will argue for our handiwork in our desire to ensure its existence, expand on its value, and improve its realization.

 High-Performance Operating System—Cornerstone 1

> **When people create something, they tend to own, protect, nurture, sustain, and fulfill it.**

This creation represents a change in our world, a change that we began and will oversee. If we produce something together in a relationship or on a team, we collectively experience the same connection to what's been created. It's ours. It's our shared goal. In some cases, such as a family, a team, or a revolution, the creation becomes our identity.

In a business (or family), not everyone will have the same opportunity to construct everything together from a blank page. Despite the different level of contribution to the original product, everyone can form a meaningful relationship to what's been created. Such a relationship is more than merely desirable; it is essential in a well-functioning environment. I may not have authored the Bill of Rights or the Ten Commandments; however, I can create a significant bond to what others have originated by developing a strong and important connection to what exists.

As you gain momentum in working through *Choose What Works* and building a new future, I will address how others whom you depend on will be able to understand and relate effectively to your vision, ideas, and projects.

STORE IN MEMORY

- Your operating system underlies everything you do.

- At our core, our relationships with each other, with ourselves, and ultimately with life are given meaning through language.

- You've begun reading *Choose What Works* for a reason. What is it?

- This book will have the most impact when you take action by collecting your authentic responses in writing where requested.

- New levels of clarity and unexpected resolve result from the simple act of getting stuff out of your head and onto paper.

- You and I have the gift of creation. The power to create comes from our words, our language, and our visions.

- When people create something, they own, protect, nurture, sustain, and fulfill it.

CHAPTER 2.0

Words Make Worlds
Accounting for the past

◆·◆

"We forget that the description is only a description, and thus, we entrap the totality of ourselves in a vicious cycle from which we rarely emerge in our lifetime."
—CARLOS CASTANEDA, AUTHOR AND ANTHROPOLOGIST

◆·◆

 Preview

2.1 **Access two worlds** The notion that we reside in a world of perception and interpretation seems normal to us. Yet, another world is within our reach. This world is brought into existence by speaking with creative intent, imagination, and precision.

2.2 **Describe or inscribe** For most of us, the difference between a result and an achievement is not pronounced. Describe or inscribe provides additional meaning in this apparently subtle distinction to build more rigorously on our theme of two worlds in which we operate.

2.3 **Results** A result arises from a worldview that holds that something actually happened. Our challenge when we speak from this viewpoint is to describe "reality" accurately. As we come to understand our worldview, we will see it as a product of our unexamined operating system and its concealed logic.

2.4 **Achievements** An achievement can refer to the same event or happening as a result. Yet an achievement exists in a different worldview or operating system that generates new possibilities and therefore new routes to the future.

2.1   Access two worlds

We live in a world of perception and interpretation that seems normal to us. We know how things "are." As a result, we have a sense of what is real and what is not. People, situations, and objects in our world have qualities that are "given." These qualities are generally accepted and rarely questioned. We also regard ourselves in ways that we seldom question beyond the obvious. Within our self-referential framework, we think we know who we are, how we feel, and what we want.

Our normal world is structured and solidified through our words, understanding, and beliefs. The resulting worldview is "known" and held in place by unconscious agreement within our own rationale and with others. As we come to understand this worldview, we will see it as a product of our unexamined operating system and its concealed logic. A primary instruction that governs its (our) operation is: *Accurately describe the real world.*

However, another world is within our reach. This world is brought into existence by speaking with creative intent, imagination, and precision.

All people, objects, and events have a reality to them. This view of reality holds that virtually everything can be described and eventually explained. Our job in this system is to "Say what is real, and get it right." Some examples of speaking descriptively within this worldview are:

- "The room is big."
- "The project is complex."
- "She is smart."
- "The program is used for drawing charts."

The key to understanding these examples as the *normal worldview* is to question the use of "is" in each case. "Big," "complex," "smart," and "used for" are values or interpretations, not absolute reality.

However, another world is within our reach. This world is brought into existence by speaking with *creative* intent, imagination, and precision. In this mode, you are able to express words, ideas, and actions that manifest new possibilities beyond those that are "given." This creative, rather than *descriptive,* system functions to free new ideas and points of view from the solidified background of unconscious agreement—the world we hold as real. The ability to discern new forms is extremely powerful as a tool for creation. A primary instruction of this operating system is the question: "What is possible?"

Allow the question "What is possible?" to evoke new views, ideas, and interpretations. Say what is *possible.* Say it so that it connects with people's values and is compelling.

If we revisit the previous examples and use a creative rather than descriptive approach, we might say the following:

- "The room could be divided to make different use of the space."
- "The project would benefit if we broke it into smaller tasks."
- "I appreciate her thoughtful contributions."
- "The program could be converted to other applications."

As you can see, I've taken the "accurate" descriptive examples from the normal worldview and expressed alternative, creative ideas. The point is to see the almost limitless range of potential ideas one can form beyond the grip of what is "given." I am highlighting *my sense of what could be,* which extends beyond what we assume to be immutable fact.

Your interest in this *created world* is to advance new, more generous concepts of what is feasible. Creative ideas that are more in line with what you really care about are foundational elements for working with a new operating system.

Your creative ideas spring from questions such as, "What's possible?" An additional question in the instruction set for a newly formulated operating system is "What do you intend?" This question held in the background of your thinking will enable you to see new and expanded opportunities.

Display 2.1 summarizes the key differences between the two world-views or operating systems that I'm addressing in this chapter.

Display 2.1   Comparison of worldviews

Worldview/ Operating System	Formative Principle	Scope of Opportunities
Normal	Unexamined acceptance	Limited
Alternative, creative	Created perspective	Expanded

Every step we'll take in *Choose What Works* is an opportunity for you to examine what you've accepted for yourself, in your world as you've currently constructed it.

Once you can see with new perceptions, you will be free to choose either to maintain a set of "given" interpretations or to create new perspectives and possibilities. Once discovered, this fertile process has unlimited applications for you in working with your newly liberated operating system.

Your authority and skill issue from your ability to choose clearly and to then act, knowing how and when to apply and balance the two systems.

Both of these worldviews, or operating systems, emerge and take form through language.

Both systems are valid. Operating with skill in the two worlds is essential for you to work sanely and effectively. If you have access to only one or the other, your responses and performance will be impoverished and limited. Your authority and skill issue from your ability to choose clearly and then to act, knowing how and when to apply and balance the two systems.

2.2   Describe or inscribe

Let's now proceed to the next step in accessing your two worlds. In *Spec Sheet 2.4*, which follows in two subchapters, I will ask you to respond to the question "What's been achieved?" But first, some background to aid you in understanding what I'm asking here.

Refer to *Display 2.2* (below). Imagine this diagram as a file you've pulled up on your computer screen. The name of the file you've retrieved is "Outcomes." I have divided the "Outcomes" file into two sections, separated horizontally. On the top we have "Result." On the bottom we have "Achievement."

For most of us, the difference between a *result* and an *achievement* is not pronounced. However, I propose to show you additional meaning in this apparently subtle distinction to build more rigorously on our theme of two worlds.

Display 2.2   Outcomes

RESULT

- A record of what's happened
- Always measured
- Objective
- Occurred in the past; it is historic
- Act of accurately describing "reality"

ACHIEVEMENT

- What you say happened, that makes a difference
- Something valued
- Subjective
- Occurred in the past yet affects the way we regard our future
- Act of creating a new perspective or possibility for others

I am defining a result as "a record of what happened."

Something happened. You, or others, experienced something. We saw, heard, or sensed something in the environment. By "record," I mean a representation, not a literal re-creation, of the occurrence we experienced. The result is simply a record of what happened. For example: They scored 4; we scored 2. That's the result: 4 to 2.

I am defining an achievement as "what you say happened that makes a difference."

An achievement can refer to the same event or happening as a result, as in the above example of "They scored 4; we scored 2." Yet an achievement exists in a different worldview, or operating system. I will present examples of achievement as we continue.

What do these carefully chosen words, "Result" and "Achievement," mean to you? Let's further define the elements that will enrich the distinction.

A result is always measured.

An achievement can be measured; however, it's characterized as something valued.

A result attempts to be objective in its depiction of reality.

An achievement is purposely subjective in its expression.

A result occurred in the past. It is historic.

An achievement, although occurring in the past, affects the way we regard the future.

(And here's where things get a little tricky.)

A result arises from a worldview that holds that something actually happened, such as "They scored 4; we scored 2." Your challenge when you speak from this viewpoint is to describe "reality" accurately.

An achievement springs from an alternative, creative worldview that maintains that speaking causes something new to be seen. Your challenge, in this realm, is to generate new possibilities. Once you speak, you create new ways for others to consider situations they may have taken for granted until now.

Now let's revisit the previous example: "They scored 4; we scored 2."

In the world of results, we interpret "4 to 2" to mean something. How do you relate to the result in this example? It's probably something like:

- "They won; we lost."
- "They were better."
- "We didn't get the job done."
- "We'll never be able to beat them."
- "They stole the game."

The string of interpretation builds on itself in an endless loop.

In the world of achievements, the conversation goes something like this: "They scored 4; we scored 2. ("They were the local professional soccer team. We were our company's pickup squad.") Specific achievements might include the following:

- "We proved to ourselves that we could play competitively with the best."
- "We raised $85,000 for charity."
- "We pulled the whole company together."
- "We had fun and forged a team spirit."

Our ability to express achievement is virtually unlimited. We are limited only by our capacity to bring forward additional points of view.

These original viewpoints are expressions of what our *commitment* allows us to *see*. For instance, in the previous example, my regard for the company team opened the possibility for each of the achievements I suggested. In other words, I select matter-of-fact, everyday elements, and I build new perspectives for others to consider. These perspectives, crafted from my commitments, can become an additional and valuable aspect of other people's reality.

Speaking achievements is part of the vocabulary of leadership. By leadership, I am not referring to a job title. I am referring to a way of seeing, and a way of creating with your words and actions.

Speaking achievements is part of the vocabulary of leadership. By leadership, I am not referring to a job title. I am referring to a way of seeing and a way of creating with your words and actions.

I didn't say that results are better than achievements. Nor did I say that achievements are better than results. If we are skilled in only one of these domains, we are operating with only half the tools. Results and achievements together represent two worlds of reality that we must come to master in our new operating system.

2.3   Results

Now let's return to developing the question I raised earlier, "What's been achieved?" To answer this question and to gain skill in expressing achievements, we need to start with results. In *Spec Sheet 2.3* I will ask you to complete the sentences indicated and express your responses as results. I then guide you, in *Spec Sheet* 2.4, to convert these results into achievements.

Remember that results are stated in measurable terms.

For example:

- "I was the leading sales rep in our district."
- "I raised two children as a single parent."
- "Our clients demonstrate the highest environmental test scores."

SPEC SHEET 2.3
DESCRIBING THE RESULTS

Write your responses to the following six questions. (Example responses are provided.)

What results have you produced:

in your current work? (1)

(Developed strategies that grew the company from $3M to $6M in annual sales)

_____

_____

in your career? (2)

(Started marketing department in two companies; received Marcom Award from industry peers)

in other areas of your life? (3)

(Happily married for nine years; two great kids)

What *results* have been produced by:

your current work colleagues? (4)

(Assisted in building company revenues by $3MM in 2 years)

your former work colleagues? (5)

(Sold our last company to larger competitor)

your customers or clients? (6)

(Three of our customers are leading their respective industries in growth)

2.4   Achievements

Great! Now using *Spec Sheet 2.4*, convert the results in your response into achievements.

First, review what you wrote in *Spec Sheet 2.3*, and then, apply the following format: "Say what's happened (the result), _____ and what it makes possible (the achievement) _____."

For example:

- "I say that being the leading sales rep in the district makes possible a career in sales management."
- "I say that raising two children as a single parent makes possible extending that character growth to other areas of self-reliance in my career."
- "I say that our customers' environmental test scores make possible our gaining recognition as the leading environmental agency in the state."

Remember that achievements are valued and make something possible as you move ahead.

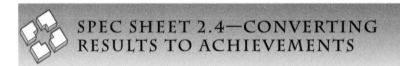

SPEC SHEET 2.4—CONVERTING RESULTS TO ACHIEVEMENTS

Convert the results in *Spec Sheet* 2.3 into achievements. Start now by responding to the following prompts. (Example responses are provided.)

I say that (refer to result in *Spec Sheet 2.3*)

(Developed strategies that grew the company from $3MM to $6MM in annual sales)

make(s) possible,

(Our leadership in the marketing services category)

_____

_____

I say that (refer to result in *Spec Sheet 2.3*)
(Started marketing department in two companies; received Marcom Award from industry peers)

_____

make(s) possible

(my candidacy as a future VP Marketing)

_____

_____

I say that (refer to result in *Spec Sheet 2.3*)

(Happily married for nine years; two great kids)

_____

_____

make(s) possible

(Guiding my children to be happy, successful people)

_____

_____

I say that (refer to result in *Spec Sheet 2.3*)

(Assisted in building company revenues by $3MM in two years)

_____

_____

make(s) possible

(Growing the company to be a $20MM firm in three years)

_____

_____

I say that (refer to result in *Spec Sheet 2.3*)

(Sold our last company to larger competitor)

_____

_____

make(s) possible

(Our recognition as a publicly traded company within three years)

_____

_____

I say that (refer to result in *Spec Sheet 2.3*)

(Three of our customers are leading their respective industries in growth)

_____

_____

make(s) possible

(That our customers can succeed with the marketing tools we provide them)

_____

_____

Notice we used the sentence stem "I say." What does that add to your expression of achievement? Most people I coach report that it establishes a strong sense of ownership. Additionally, the words that follow *I say* when you speak are received by your audience as an assertion—a compelling claim that doesn't require support of evidence.

In making such assertions, you empower yourself and engage your audience through the innovation of consciously selected language. Your achievements are announced without disclaimers like:

- "I think ..."
- "My feeling is ..."
- "You may disagree, but ..."

How does it feel to express yourself in the world of achievement? What do you notice about your feelings? What is your sense of the experience of others?

"I like the dreams of the future better than the history of the past."

—THOMAS JEFFERSON, THIRD PRESIDENT OF THE UNITED STATES

"Positive," "proud," and "upbeat" are the kinds of adjectives I hear most often. You've shifted the tone and quality of how you are regarded. Your enthusiasm contributes energy and interest in your interactions with others.

Speaking results and achievements creates a *platform* on which to build new routes to the future. The landscape for that construction and the road map and tools required to transcend your past are what we will turn our attention to next.

STORE IN MEMORY

- Our normal world is structured and solidified through our words, understanding, and beliefs.

- A primary instruction that governs its (our) operation is: "Accurately describe the real world."

- However, another world is within our reach. This world is brought into existence by speaking with creative intent, imagination, and precision.

- Creative ideas that are more in line with what you really care about are foundational elements for working with a new operating system.

- Every step we'll take in *Choose What Works* is an opportunity for you to examine what you've accepted for yourself in your world, as you've currently constructed it.

- A result is "a record of what happened."

- An achievement springs from an alternative, creative worldview that maintains that speaking causes something new to be *seen*. Your challenge, in this realm, is to generate new possibilities.

- Speaking about achievements is part of the vocabulary of leadership.

- In making such assertions, you empower yourself and engage your audience through the innovation of consciously selected language.

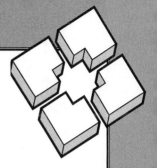

CHAPTER 3.0

Default Settings
Observing what you can't see

◆·◆

"If knowledge can create problems, it is not through
ignorance that we can solve them."

—ISAAC ASIMOV, AUTHOR

◆·◆

 Preview

3.1 **In the *Mood*** Moods are variable. They can be shifted through
your conscious action. First, though, you have to understand
what happened to set up the mood. Then you can move with
suitable tools to alter your environment.

3.2 **What's created when you speak?** What is said and how others
interpret and react to that input collectively produce these
moods and resultant conditions.

3.3 **What's created when you listen?** Far more elusive is observing
how we listen to the world. I am talking about how you pay
attention to the world, how you analyze, assess, and observe.

3.4 **You're not a *blank disk*** The primary way we listen to the world
is through a set of filters. These filters act as default subtexts for
changes or perceived threats in our environment.

3.5 **The right problems** Our problems are troubling and upsetting
when we are enmeshed in their grip. We can also understand problems as interpretations coded in our Default Operating System.

3.6 **It vs. you** Our problems happen to us in ways in which we perceive ourselves as victims. The circumstances—other people,
other events, other situations—impose themselves on us.

3.1   In the *Mood*

We work in an environment. By environment, I'm not talking about the color of the walls or the style of the furniture. Rather, I'm referring specifically to the *mood* or atmosphere in which we function.

At work, for example, we operate in a collective mood, composed of the spoken and unspoken thoughts and feelings of people with whom we come in contact. Most people can sense the mood beneath the organizational veneer, whether a small firm or a large company. Pervasive and larger than any individual, the mood can predetermine how you feel, what you think, and, ultimately, what you do. The mood can be of high energy, of enthusiasm, or the opposite—grim determination, or worse, the resignation of complete cynicism.

Imagine you've worked for weeks to complete a critical project. You've made untold sacrifices to meet the deadline. When you deliver the project, you hear some ritual "thank you's," but then the next "emergency" occurs to grind you and your colleagues. A deadening, possibly suppressive mood descends.

Conversely, we regard other work situations with a special fondness. In these formative experiences, people are there for us, to challenge, lift, and inspire us beyond where we thought we could perform. An enlivening, buoyant mood prevails.

Mood is an important element that I work to identify and reestablish when I begin working with a group of people. If possible, I arrange to meet prospective clients at their office. In the first few minutes, while I wait in the reception area, I go through a mental checklist:

- How was I greeted?
- How does the receptionist answer the phone and handle inquiries?
- Do the people I see appear alert? Are they excited?
- Is the green plant in the corner flourishing or wilted?
- Is the area organized, clean, and welcoming?

The mood affects and can be detected in every aspect of the life of the business. Just as an observer barely views changes slowly happening in a tropical fish tank, when the water gets darker in the preverbal organizational tank, it does so gradually. All are immersed in an almost imperceptivity changing system. Pinpointing the mood can be hard for those inside the system. However, others who work outside of the silent agreement of those unconscious pacts, and are awake to such impressions, can often readily sense them.

Moods have as much of an effect on our personal relationships and our families as on our work lives. Think what it would be like to have an unresolved spat with your spouse or partner and then set out to plan your summer vacation. It's hard to invest much passion in the planning when your enthusiasm is blunted by unexpressed emotion.

The result of a shift in mood can be dramatic as it affects people's actions. I have witnessed individuals working within a group "go away." They appear to lose contact with the thread of the discussion, become "unresponsive," and stop actively participating. Sometimes, what was said that triggered the retreat is obvious. In other cases, what happened to drive an individual or a group off course is more difficult to detect. Step one is to observe that something changed. Then, we can discover its cause.

Before you proceed to develop ideas and plans to build your future, it is important to understand the conditions in which you and others around you are operating. Ask yourself the following three questions as a guide to revealing the mood around you and what brings it on:

- What is the dominant mood where you work? (Examples: excitement, threat, boredom, anticipation)
- What mood characterizes your relationship to your "boss" or other influential relationships in your work and life? (Examples: Intimidation, warmth, playfulness, suppression, anger)
- What usually happens at your work to change people's levels of energy, interest, and involvement, for the better or worse? (Examples: sales results announced, new projects assigned, the weekend, jokes at the water cooler)

Moods are variable. They can be shifted through your conscious action. First, though, you have to understand what happened to set up the mood. Then, you can move to alter your environment once you are equipped with suitable tools and reliable techniques. I'll be supplying you with these as we move through *Choose What Works*.

3.2   What's created when you speak?

What is said and how others interpret and react to that input collectively produces these moods and resultant conditions. As a first step in revealing the impact of your words on the prevailing mood and reactions of others, consider what's created when you speak.

Candidly reflect on following three questions:

- How often are you willing to step back and examine the chain of cause and effect shaping your most important relationships at work and in your personal life?
- When do you complicate or prolong difficult situations with your reactions or opinions?
- What do you invite and make possible by speaking?

Speaking is "verbal math." What you say is a type of equation in the environment of your relationships. The sum of your words equals the reactions that occur in your life. The equation is composed of what you say and how listeners receive it, with mood and emotional tone as the carriers. Your reactions and the reactions of others generate emotional tone in the relationship. I call this emotional tone a localized mood in the domain of your relationships. *Display 3.2a* (see page 29) illustrates this relationship calculus.

Speaking is "verbal math." The sum of your words equals the reactions that occur in your life.

Certain ways of speaking build connection. Some forms of talk produce clarity, understanding, and agreement. These types of conversation evoke action and coordination. However, other talk falls short of the mark. It creates resistance and confusion and leaves you and others frustrated and judgmental.

Display 3.2a   The Verbal Math equation

Sum of your words ➕ Mood/emotional tone ═ Reactions that occur

Installing the skills of effective speaking requires *scrutiny* and *discipline*. Scrutiny is accomplished by honestly reviewing what you say and its impact on the people receiving your communication. Discipline requires your relentless integrity in overriding forms of expression that condemn you to self-justified habits of interaction. You can't just attach a loudspeaker to your random thoughts and reactions and expect your audience to sort out your intent and message. Start now by noticing what you say. To become more effective, ask yourself the following questions when communicating or reviewing discussions:

- What do I intend in this situation?
- What does my listener care about?
- Did my words reflect my intent?
- Is what I said accurate?
- Is what I said true? And how do I know it's true?
- Am I connecting with my audience? How do I know?
- Was what I said received as I intended? How do I know this?
- What was moved forward or deepened in this conversation? (For instance: commitments, understanding, friendship, trust, suspicion, confusion)

Reflect on these points in the background of the conversations you conduct. As you work through these questions, you will begin to acquire the insights and linguistic tools to navigate successfully in your new system of operation.

When a client of mine first read these questions, he reported that he couldn't bring himself to speak for five days. Maybe he was exaggerating, but what he noticed shocked him. He realized that much of what he thought and spoke was, in his words, "bullshit." He was a smart, accomplished guy, respected by the people with whom he worked and lived. However, when he took these questions to heart and consistently observed his daily interactions, he recognized that much of his communication was inaccurate and limiting—or worse, insulting.

My client saw with a new sense of clarity that common expressions he used produced reactions in his audience that he never "intended." These reactions, like subtle forms of resistance, revealed that the way he communicated was regularly misunderstood or misinterpreted as arrogant or egotistical. Particular expressions that many of us use evoke surprising reactions, including argument and a lack of affinity. Here's a sampling:

- "You should"
- "You ought to"
- "You must"
- "You are"
- "I can't"
- "You can't"
- "I need you to"

These speech forms appear inoffensive enough; however, look over the list carefully. When you go beyond the conventions that most of us take for granted, you begin to see the manipulation, coercion, and lack of respect embedded in such commonplace phrases.

As a next step in the progress of my client, I asked him whether he was willing to go past explaining and justifying why and how he used these and other expressions. He wanted to improve his effectiveness and others' regard for him. In moving forward, I showed him the traps of his *default system* language and outlined alternative ways to redesign his approach to others. I coached him how to design more specifically and precisely what he said to increase the likelihood of people acting affirmatively toward his intent.

He followed his commitment to show others more respect by redesigning his interactions with them: "I suggest" replaced "You ought to," "You are" became "You acted in ways that," and "I need you to" was recast as "Will you?" These subtle yet thoughtful and deliberate changes in his speaking produced a dramatic shift in how others regarded him. The responses he invited when he interacted with his staff were profound. In a period of six months, he was recognized in an internal company poll as the having the highest retention rate of key employees and was noted for his ability to attract critical hires.

Display 3.2b (below) lists the new ways my client was able to express himself in line with his desire to respect others and using his *verbal math* skills.

Display 3.2b   "Verbal Math" choices

Customary expressions	Alternative *choices* to build respect and evoke action
■ "You should"	"Please consider"
■ "You ought to"	"I suggest"
■ "You must"	"I request that you"
■ "You are"	"You acted in ways that"
■ "I can't"	"I am currently not willing/able to"
■ "You can't"	"I ask that you do not"
■ "I need you to"	"Will you?"

When prompted, we can begin to come to terms with what we put into the mix through our speaking. Doing so requires a willingness to see what's happening outside our momentary point of view. The place to stand while making this observation is what I call *being responsible.* The stand we take for being responsible acts as a platform for accessing and maintaining your new operating system.

3.3   What's created when you listen?

Sure, in most cases, you can be responsible for what you say. This level of responsibility qualifies you as an adult. Far more elusive is observing how we listen to the world. By *listening*, I don't mean the mechanics of using the little bones in your middle ear to hear. Rather, I am talking about how you pay attention to the world, how you analyze and assess and observe. This interior practice involves how you interpret what's happening and the range of responses you have to that *input*.

By listening, I am referring to your awareness to what you pay attention. I offer two questions to promote your personal insight:

1. What is the conversation you conduct with the world?
2. What is the internal process that focuses and filters your attention?

What is the conversation you conduct with the world?

The first question addresses our internal dialogue that is constantly running, even though the "mute" button is usually pressed. This dialogue is omnipresent, and therefore, we seldom acknowledge or "hear" it. Our conversation with the world has a pattern with recurring themes. We are not simply objective journalists reporting on the ongoing stream of events, people, and impressions. What is the conversation you conduct with the world? How does it differ from the internal conversation of others? In what ways is it similar?

What is the conversation you conduct with the world?

The Buddhists have a saying about our mysterious nature that comments on the apparent sightlessness of three species:

- "Fish are blind to water."
- "Birds are blind to air."
- "Humans are blind to themselves."

Like fish and birds, we reside in an omnipresent medium. In our case, we are immersed and surrounded by our subjective explanation of our movement through life. We are blind to ourselves: our self-limiting routines, our processes of thought, and very often the ways we appear on the *display screen* of other people's perception.

What is the internal process that focuses and filters your attention?

Now let's examine the second question. Once you start sensing your inner dialogue more often, you may notice recognizable configurations of thought. What are these recurring themes? For now, let's say they are dominated by our reactions. On closer examination, many of these reactions are predictable and mechanistic. They recur automatically. I'll call these reactions "having thoughts."

Here's an illustration: "Don't think of pink elephants with black polka dots." Okay, you have an immediate image displayed internally of pink elephants, even though the instruction was not to think of them. Who's doing the thinking here? Whose thoughts are they? What is the mechanism of control and volition? When I speak of reactions, I'm referring to this automatic mechanism. How often do you have similar reactions in the current of everyday interactions? To what degree do you misidentify these reactions as the product of your thinking?

> "When we talk about thinking, we are concerned with opening a new future, and producing a future other than the future that will arrive to us out of inertia."
> —Fernando Flores, Philosopher and Entrepreneur

These *reactive thoughts* are distinct from what I am asking you to regard as *thinking,* a process that is reflective, creative, and enlivening. Thinking in this sense relates to our ability to engage innovatively and productively in our ongoing dialogue with life. What's at stake is the future that these discernible inner processes produce. Reactive thoughts yield a predictably recurring future. *Creative thinking* generates the possibility of new tomorrows. *Display 3.3* (see page 34) summarizes the two approaches to our dialogue with the world.

Sufficient reflection on the questions I've raised about the nature and focus of your discourse with the world is essential for you to identify your existing operating system. When you know the system you've been working with, you will be free to apply an alternate system that will deliver your highest levels of performance.

Something is created in the conversations that you conduct within your world. It can be far more powerful than just the words you

Display 3.3   Reactive Thoughts vs. Creative Thinking

Inner dialogue	Characteristics	Output
"Having thoughts"	Reactive, mechanistic, automatic	Future based on recurring past
"Thinking"	Reflective, creative, enlivening	New futures

speak. The way others listen to you is instructive here. Have you ever noticed that with some of your friends, you are smarter and with others, you are funnier, sexier, more articulate, or optimistic? How do you explain this?

The differences have to do with the regard that your respective friends have for you. This predetermined view is a positive judgment about you. It is the milieu of thought into which you are speaking. The conversation surrounding you has an interactive and influential quality that shapes your thinking and behavior. Your friends are granting you freedom to express an aspect of yourself that is not always predominant.

The best managers I know and admire speak to people as capable, intelligent, and responsible. They are often willing to confer these qualities to people before the fact. They are generous in that that they speak to "what's great" in others. In most cases, people respond with actions that are consistent with the qualities these managers extend to them.

Three examples demonstrate extending qualities to people before the "evidence":

- "I know you'll do a brilliant job."
- "I'm sure you're already familiar with these ideas."
- "I know this is something that you care about."

In personal relationships, you can see a similar effect. Your friends' judgments condition them to interact with you in ways that match their view of you. You reciprocate with behavior that is consistent with the *subtext* that underlies the relationship. This subtext is the unspoken belief that governs your interaction. You are smarter, funnier, and sexier in the tacit *code* of this system. Of course, if others attend to us in negative terms, we suppress our self-expression. When our natural instincts are blunted, our reaction is to withdraw or to exaggerate our behavior. Being overly "nice" is an example of a reaction to a perceived threat.

We operate within the *bandwidth* provided by others. We also operate in the bandwidth we are willing to grant to ourselves.

When I worked in the entertainment business, I noticed with amazement that some performers were able to "fill up the space" that resulted from the adoring praises of fans and critics. The performing artists became as brilliant and talented as people claimed they were in spite of the artists' own very human considerations about their "star" qualities.

Others entertainers I observed withdrew from the edge of celebrity, out of overwhelming concerns for their ability to replicate their initial success. In some cases, they lacked the reassuring connection with their audience. Their talent seemed to wither as their self-confidence was thwarted by criticism or misunderstanding of the direction of their work.

We operate within the *bandwidth* provided by others. We also operate in the bandwidth we are willing to grant to ourselves. In the final analysis, when we are willing to release ourselves from our own judgments, we are freed from the boundaries ascribed by others.

In *Spec Sheet 3.3,* which follows, you have an opportunity to reveal to yourself the existing subtexts that underlie your relationships. Once you have identified the actual subtext existing in each relationship, you can create a new *context*. You can consciously craft a new frame of reference to support these relationships in the future.

An example of a subtext in relation to your "boss" is: "You have the power to fire me. I need your approval to feel good about my future at the company." If you're a "boss," you may want to extend this question of relating to your customers or clients. Of course, confronting the subtext, which is the basic way of relating to this person who organizes most of your interactions, may not be easy.

When you have identified the operative subtext, you can then intentionally create the context that you desire for the relationship. Continuing with the above example, you could now say to yourself something like: "I will work professionally and to the best of my abilities. I trust that my value will be evident to you and others throughout the company." This context holds the promise of changing your relationship to your "boss" from fearful reaction to respect for the relationship and for yourself.

SPEC SHEET 3.3
SUBTEXTS TO CONTEXTS

In the space provided, identify the existing subtext and author the desired context in the following relationships that you have: (Example responses are provided.)

with specific individuals at work (name person and the existing subtext)

(John, boss: I can never seem to please you)
_____

_____

_____

(the desired context is)

(I appreciate the quality of your work and the contribution you make)
_____

_____

_____

with your friends/colleagues (name person and the existing subtext)

(Peter: Why can't you be more like me?)
_____

_____

(the desired context is)

(I appreciate you for who you are)
_____

_____

with family members (name person and the existing subtext)

(Sue, sister: we are always competing to be the best)
_____

_____

(the desired context is)

(We are both great, let's appreciate and support each other)
_____

_____

with yourself (the existing subtext is)

(I am never satisfied with my results)
_____

_____

(the desired context is)

(I am doing great and will continue to grow beyond who and where I am today)
_____

_____

3.4   You're not a *blank disk*

Our unexamined subtexts filter virtually every relationship and point of view. This screening activity is not random. Rather, it has a pattern of surprising consistency, which I will reveal to you. If we can view the underlying logic of other people, we gain great insight into their existing operating systems and, by extension, our own.

The primary way we listen to the world is through a set of *filters.* These filters act as *default subtexts* for changes or perceived threats in our environment:

- What changes are occurring (or will occur)?
- How does what's happening or being said affect me?
- Is this good or bad for me (or whom I identify with)?

These ever-present filters are driven by primary human concerns for security, safety, and survival. These filters are part of the *logic* of our *default operating system.* The logic goes like this: (see *Display 3.4*)

Display 3.4   Our reaction to change/threat

 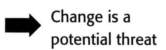 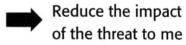

Something's changing ➡ Change is a potential threat ➡ Reduce the impact of the threat to me

The *logic* can apply to you individually or to a group with which you identify. Instances of group identification can extend to an organization, a religious group, a military unit, your gender, or your family. The logic is pervasive and has the *priority command* in your default operating system. You and I don't have to operate the keys and dials because the logic of our reactive thought functions on autopilot.

In common language we express this reactive logic in simple, judgmental couplets:

- What we agree with / what we argue against

- What we like / what we don't like
- Where we must win / how we must avoid losing
- When must we always be right / when must we make what is threatening wrong
- Which explanations support our point of view / which justifications deflect criticism from us

Unlike a blank disk, we're not on "standby" to receive the undistorted imprint of the world. We're already filled with recorded memories, preferences, and critical assessments in the internal *storage* of our operating system. Sorting and retrieving our screened history serves to reinforce our points of view. These filtered experiences, forged in the past, form our core beliefs. Others in our life come to regard this *system* in more pragmatic terms. They call it "you."

Since your assessment and response worked so well in the original threatening event, you unconsciously adapted the behavior to all similar subsequent events. The code was silently written on the master program. Thus, you created your default operating system.

If you are quietly protesting "But I'm not like that," you're demonstrating my point perfectly. You see, the *logic system* is continually at work, structuring our reactions. In this case, your protest validates the coupled logic "What we agree with / what we argue against."

Your automatic filter governing your responses to private disturbances and social alarms was set early in your experience. Let's say you formed one of the above judgments in some situation that you felt was critical to your perceived safety. Since your assessment and response worked so well in the original threatening event, you unconsciously adapted the behavior to all similar subsequent events. The code was silently written on the master program. Thus, you created your default operating system.

Fortunately, you have the option of overriding the default operating system. I will show you how when we talk about *Focused Intent*, later in *Choose What Works*. For now, it's important that you appreciate the persistence and power of the default settings. These settings, which administer your responses, were put in place through the reactive logic of your default operating system. Left unmanaged, they will determine the scope of your future experience.

Display 3.4a (see page 41) illustrates the scope or bandwidth of our default operating system versus the *High-Performance Operating System*™. The diagram displays how we relate to what's happening in the default mode of experience and in the High-Performance mode.

The top of *Display 3.4a* shows the effect of your "Default Operating System" on the way you relate to current opportunities. Its limited bandwidth is derived from and set by previous experience. The full range of *"What's happening or Being Said"* goes unperceived. The mechanism is exclusive and limits new interpretations and creative responses. The resulting output is reduced experience and fewer possibilities.

On the bottom we see the expansive bandwidth of your "High-Performance Operating System." Your listening for *"What's Happening or Being Said"* is inclusive and generative. In this mode, you can creatively interact with what's occurring. The benefit of the High-Performance Operating System allows you to perceive additional possibilities and create new opportunities.

"To live a creative life, we must lose our fear of being wrong."
—JOSEPH CHILTON PEARCE, AUTHOR AND EDUCATOR

As we proceed in *Choose What Works*, we will continue to enrich and develop the body of distinctions that characterize both the default and High-Performance Operating Systems.

3.5   The right problems

Problems appear as real. More precisely, our problems are troubling and upsetting when we are enmeshed in their grip. Although this is undoubtedly our experience, we can also understand problems as interpretations coded in our default operating system. Let's explore our relationship to problems, starting with the default settings that we linked to them.

Display 3.4a   Bandwidths: Default vs. High-Performance Operating Systems

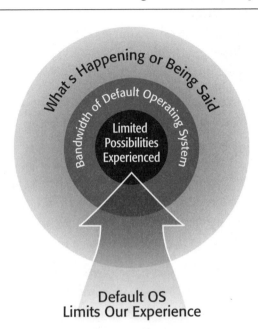

Default OS
Limits Our Experience

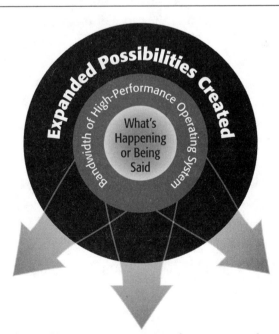

High-Performance OS Expands Our Experience

Problems exist in relation to your wants, desires, and intents. They occur when something or someone thwarts your desires or aims that reside in the background of your thoughts. In this sense, a problem is something that "shouldn't be."

Examples of problems include the following:

- (Your aim) You have a 15-minute drive to reach an important meeting, but (something happened) your tire goes flat.
- (Your aim) You need to close a large contract this month, but (something happened) your firm is not selected.
- (Your aim) You have attempted repeatedly to contact someone important, but (something happened) this person has not returned your calls and e-mails.

You and I can relate to these common upsetting events. These all qualify as problems because the incident (something happened) thwarts the background desire (your aim). We interpret the connection between our existing desire and the current incident as the cause of the problem.

A problem is something that "shouldn't be."

The actual event (flat tire, lost sale, no reply) and the background aim (get to meeting, make quota, reach important person) are now fused in our *reactive logic* by the conversation we have built. If we separate the linkage we created between the background aim and the incident, something interesting emerges. Let's see how a problem, seen in this light, starts to release its emotional grip.

If we simply change the word "but" to "and" in our examples, we begin to see how we might grasp the problem differently. Take the first example:

- (Your aim) You have a 15-minute drive to reach an important meeting, and (something happened) your tire goes flat.

"The problem is not that there are problems. The problem is expecting otherwise and thinking that having problems is a problem."

—THEODORE RUBIN,
PSYCHIATRIST AND AUTHOR

Now the default logic, which locks together cause and effect with the word "but," has been separated with "and." Something happened, and you have an existing aim. You are now able to see points of view, and possible solutions, outside of the conditions that bound your reactions to the incident.

By objectifying your "problems," you are able to employ an alternative and more effective logic. In the default perspective, your problems occur as personal and unfairly cruel.

- Consider that the flat tire you have is not necessarily a problem for the person driving by in the other direction. Perhaps your flat tire is vaguely interesting for that person, but it's not his or her problem.
- Your problem in not closing business isn't a problem for the firm that won the business. Perhaps they will empathize but not lose sleep.
- The person not returning your calls and e-mails is probably not worrying about your response.

Problems can overwhelm us until we detach their linguistic hooks that rule our perception. The practical implementation of this uncoupling goes far beyond semantic speculation:

- If we stand back from the grip of the problem, we can see where the problem is rooted.
- If we distinguish *what we think must happen* from *what did happen*, we can decouple these two elements in our internal logic.
- If we see something that happened as separated from the curse of "shouldn't be," we are simply left with what happened.

I'm sure that you, like the rest of us, want a quick recipe to fix your problems. Be patient. I will equip you to distinguish "what shouldn't be" from "what happened" as you apply your High-Performance Operating System. What's important now is to be able to see your problems in a different light.

3.6   It vs. you

The "shouldn't be" of our problems is related to our sense that they are *circumstantially imposed.* Our problems happen to us in ways in which we perceive ourselves as victims. The circumstances—other people, other events, other situations—impose themselves on us. Take these examples:

- "Somebody rained on my parade."
- "We were robbed by the umpire."
- "The recession drove us out of business."

Display 3.6a, Circumstantially Imposed Problems (see opposite), illustrates this dilemma.

In this subtext, the circumstances are to blame. The rain, the umpire, and the recession are the problem. However, another order for relating to problems is possible; I call it the self-generated approach.

In this self-generated frame of reference, you see clearly that you have created a challenging ambition. A conscious choice about your future, your aspiration becomes a context for how you act and for what happens—

Examples:

- "I am going to qualify for the state championship."
- "I plan to be head of the department in two years."
- "My desire is to start a business before I'm 35."

These examples are new futures that you bring into existence by declaring their possibility. They are *self-generated contexts* for where you are headed. Within the scope of your declared aspiration, you have also opened the fertile field of problems that could happen in pursuit of your goal.

Display 3.6a   Circumstantially Imposed Problems

Circumstantially Imposed Problems:

- "Shouldn't be ..."
- Sense of obligation/burden
- Resistance

In the early stages of building my consulting company and coaching practice, I hired a consultant to provide an experienced view and accelerate my progress. This individual began his coaching by asking me to respond to a host of questions detailing what my work and life would look like in 10 years. The questions included:

- What would I be spending my time on?
- How much did I want to travel and work abroad?
- What did I want to learn?
- What problems would I encounter in the course of fulfilling my dreams?

I wrote my answers to these questions on a piece of paper, discussed my ideas and aspirations with my mentor, and casually filed the form away. I then went to work on my business and life in what seemed was a "take it one day at a time" approach. The coaching lasted about nine months and was useful.

After five years, I came across my "wish list" in some back files. I was astonished to discover that I had accomplished most of what was on my 10-year horizon in fewer than five years. I was struck with how completely I had recorded what I intended to accomplish. I had not planned my route there in any detail, nor had I anticipated specific potential problems I would face. However, I was clear that the road leading to my goals would be paved with unforeseen adventures and a host of difficulties. I had envisioned a frame of reference for my future that included, rather than excluded, the potential of problems.

Let's refer to an earlier example of a challenging ambition: "I am going to qualify for the state championship." Everything that now happens to thwart our progress toward qualifying will be a problem, to be sure. However, in this context, problems are seen as a natural consequence of a powerful choice you made about your future. You took a *stand* regarding yourself and the state championships.

In the process of taking that stand, you put your future at risk. Anything could happen; there are no guarantees. You will always experience problems. However, they will occur for you in a domain that you can own and for which you can be responsible. You will have developed a radically new relationship to the problems that will inevitably occur.

Display 3.6b, Self-generated contexts (see page 47), provides an alternative experience of our relationship to problems.

I'll summarize what we've established: A self-generated context in your High-Performance Operating System is a frame of reference that you create. Such a context has the following features:

- It is created by you and consists of your intentions.
- It gives meaning to how you will regard issues that will arise within this context.
- It provides a clear background against which relevant action can now occur.
- It represents a choice you make. Your responses to future events can be consistent with that choice.
- It leads to inevitable "problems" for which you can take responsibility.

Display 3.6b   Self-Generated Contexts

Self-Generated Contexts

- Created/owned/choosen

- Gives meaning to *problems*

- Freedom for action

You create the potential for these problems when you commit to a high-performance future. If you want to reduce problems, reduce your ambition. The greater your aspiration, the more the potential for problems increases. Lower your ambition, and most problems will also evaporate. Say you don't want success, say you don't want friendships, say you don't want high vitality, and a whole host of issues go away. What you can count on, though, is that they will be replaced by an array of other problems that may not be too interesting in the final analysis.

Here is a situation that many of us can relate to that illustrates the relationship of risk and the experience of being alive. Imagine going to the racetrack to watch the Kentucky Derby. You can experience the day in at least two ways:

> "To be sure, a human being is a finite being, and his freedom is restricted. It is not freedom from conditions, but freedom to take a stand toward the conditions."
>
> —VICTOR FRANKL, PSYCHIATRIST AND HOLOCAUST SURVIVOR

- Sit in the sun, enjoy lunch in the clubhouse, and watch all the gorgeous horses and beautiful people.
- Put $500 on a horse to win.

The content of the day will be the same: horses, people, pageantry. However, placing a large bet will focus your attention and quicken your pulse. You will have something at stake in the outcome. You will be invested in the afternoon in ways that are qualitatively different from those of a casual observer.

What you are willing to risk in your career, in your passions, and in your relationships largely determines the quality of your life.

What you are willing to risk in your career, in your passions, and in your relationships largely determines the quality of your life. Declaring your future in terms of what's at stake is not comfortable. It is, however, enlivening. What exciting future are you willing to take risks for?

Replacing circumstantially imposed subtexts with powerful contexts of our choosing is one of the primary actions in the High-Performance Operating System. It's a shift of worlds, of operating platforms, and the quality of living.

Leadership, the way you engage with life, is about creating the "right" problems for you and others to work on. It's about selecting where to go to work that is consistent with your intentions. Grappling with the questions and exercises in the book is one way of being responsible for your self-generated leadership.

What will be accelerated in your life as you read, absorb, and work through *Choose What Works*? You will be guided in the development of your leadership and your ambitions in subsequent chapters.

STORE IN MEMORY

- Moods are variable. They can be shifted through your conscious action. First, though, you have to understand what happened to set up the mood in the first place.

- Speaking is "verbal math." What you say is a type of equation in the environment of your relationships. The sum of your words equals the reactions that occur in your life.

- Installing the skills of effective speaking requires scrutiny and discipline. Start now by noticing what you say.

- How you listen to the world involves how you interpret what's happening and the range of responses you have to that input.

- Our unexamined subtexts filter virtually every relationship and point of view. The primary way we listen is through the filter "How does what's happening affect me?"

- Your default operating system was set early in your experience. It was formed through your assessments and responses that worked so well in past threatening events. You unconsciously adapted these behaviors to all similar subsequent events.

- Problems exist in relation to your wants, desires, and intents. They occur when something or someone thwarts your desires or aims that reside in the background of your thoughts.

- Our problems happen to us in ways in which we perceive ourselves as victims. The circumstances—other people, other events, other situations—impose themselves on us.

- Leadership, the way you engage with life, is about creating the "right" problems to work on.

CHAPTER 4.0

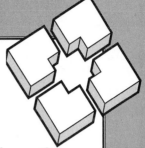

What Are You Building?
Choosing your focus and its impact

"Concentration is the secret of strengths in politics, in war, in trade, in short in all management of human affairs."
—RALPH WALDO EMERSON, PHILOSOPHER AND POET

 Preview

4.1 Everything starts with this question Your ability to respond energetically to the question "What are you building?" holds the promise of shaping your plans and your future actions.

4.2 Your focus and its impact Your statement of Focused Intent is the navigation point you will use to build additional elements of accomplishment driven by your High-Performance Operating System.

4.3 Out of your mouth Communicate your Focused Intent at first to people you think will be supportive. Tell them to listen carefully and not react until you have fully developed the possibilities that you see with them.

4.4 "What" before "how" It is important to maintain the distinction between what objectives you've set and how you and others will work toward the completion of those ends.

4.1   Everything starts with this question

"What are you building?" In the course of our lives, this is the most basic and persistent question we address. Only in recent human history have some of us had the luxury of being able to ask such a question with the expectation of latitude in how we might respond. Previously, most people had few options: they toiled through the burden of existence, their lives restricted by closed boundaries and set expectations.

"What are you building?" As you compose your response, reflect on these related questions:

- Beyond the obvious and predictable in my life, what's possible?
- What would my career look like if my dreams were realized?
- What environment could I create that would allow me to work at something about which I'm passionate?
- What professional and personal relationships am I seeking?
- What future do I want for my family and myself?

Consider what you are building in light of the following parable:

> Three individuals are laboring side by side at a large construction site. From outward appearances, they are all doing the same work. A passer-by approaches the first laborer and asks, "What are you doing?"
>
> He replies, "I'm laying bricks."
>
> The person moves along and says to the second worker, "What are you doing?"
>
> He responds, "I'm constructing a wall."
>
> The questioner walks to the third laborer, who appears to be working just like the others. The question is repeated, "What are you doing?"
>
> "I'm building a cathedral," the bricklayer says quietly.

"The important thing is this: To be willing at any moment to sacrifice what we believe ourselves to be, for what we could become."

—CHARLES DUBOIS,
SOCIAL ACTIVIST

Your ability to respond energetically to the question "What are you building?" holds the promise of shaping your plans and your future actions. Your answer becomes your frame of reference in a High-Performance Operating System that will guide your reactions and your ability to tolerate setbacks. As the third bricklayer's response implies, your answer will also become an enduring source of personal and professional satisfaction.

In Chapter 1.0, I asked you to state your expectations in reading and working through *Choose What Works*. Now, I'll direct you to shape those expectations into a coherent statement that expresses what you are building. Examples of such statements are:

I am building:
- (I will own) my own business.
- (I will become) a partner in the firm.
- (I will become) a professional travel writer.
- (We will own) our own home and have three children.

Capture what you are building in a single sentence. Compare two or three versions, and see what feels right and holds the biggest potential for you. Remember, you are not stuck with what you initially come up with. The statement is part of an ongoing process that has lots of room for revision and refinement.

I am building (I will)

_____

_____

_____

4.2   Your focus and its impact

What you are building is your broad statement of desired achievement. It's the starting point to forming a declared future, a vision of what you want to achieve. As you focus and shape this declaration, it becomes a statement of *Focused Intent,* which acts as the primary driver for your High-Performance Operating System.

We will work through all the steps required to develop your Focused Intent as we proceed. At this stage of the process, we can define a statement of Focused Intent as the following:

- It states an outcome you will attain.
- The Focused Intent addresses the "what," as opposed to the "how" your outcome will be accomplished. We will cover how you will accomplish the *intent* in Chapter 6.0.
- The "what" is measurable. The measure is not necessarily stated in the concise frame of the statement.
- The Focused Intent covers a time frame of between six months and two years. Although the time specified is variable, it is most useful to have the outcome occur in the near to midterm. I call this a "line of sight goal," as opposed to an amorphous dream. If the time frame becomes too extended, your focus is diffused and is subject to many circumstantial factors.
- The Focused Intent also takes account of the impact of the outcome on your larger vision or sense of accomplishment for the future.

Here's some examples of a statement of Focused Intent:

- *"To attain my MBA degree in the next two years so that I have the skills to be a senior marketing executive."*
- *"To start my own business within the next 12 months so that I can operate as an independent business person and triple my income."*
- *"To double my revenue over the next year so that my business is positioned to compete with the top national firms."*

The above statements fit into the following template. This structure will assist you as you compose your statement of Focused Intent:

To ("generate," "produce," "attain"—this action verb is the "what" of the statement) _____

_____

_____

_____ by _____

(timeframe) _____

so that (this is the impact of the *"what"* on a larger vision or accomplishment) _____

_____

_____

As you can see, your statement of Focused Intent describes an *outcome* you seek and its impact, expressed as a broader achievement. It is a "line of sight" foreseeable goal, which concretely states a specific result in a planned time frame. This outcome will occur within the larger context of what you are building.

Now, focus and shape your own statement of Focused Intent in *Spec Sheet 4.2*. Use the statement of *what you are building* that you developed in the previous section as the basis for conforming to the structured template provided.

SPEC SHEET 4.2
YOUR FOCUSED INTENT

In the space provided, craft your statement of *Focused Intent:* (Example responses are provided.)

To (the "what")

(start my own marketing business)

_____ **by [time frame]***(by 12/30/05)*

_____

_____

so that (impact of the "what")

(so that I can realize my dream of professional freedom)

_____

_____

Your statement of Focused Intent is the navigation point you will use to build additional elements of accomplishment driven by your High-Performance Operating System. It is the vehicle you have created to frame your choices and responses to what life presents.

4.3   Out of your mouth

Initially, the audience for your statement of Focused Intent is yourself. If you've created it or refined it in a group or small team, then the statement is for the benefit of all the members.

I ask that you make one slight modification to the statement of Focused Intent at this point. Change the first word of the statement from "To (attain, etc.)" to "I will." For example:

> *"I will attain my MBA degree in the next two years*
> *so that I have the skills to be a senior marketing executive."*

So what's the difference? Rewording the statement of Focused Intent to "I will" affirms authorship and ownership and a commitment to perform. By altering your statement to read "I will," you have taken a stand for yourself and your future which you have now declared.

Practice communicating the Focused Intent alone at first. See whether you can get the statement out of your mouth without any disempowering disclaimers such as:

- "I'm not really sure about this, but ..."
- "You may feel otherwise; however ..."
- "I came up with a new idea about what I want"

You can, of course, share your statement of Focused Intent with others. This is your first test. However, take care to whom you reveal it and what you say. It may well be premature to share it at this stage, as it is likely still extremely fragile. Without adequate preparation and additional substance, others' critical or selfishly misdirected views could be damaging.

Communicate at first with people you think will be supportive, people who view you and your achievements in an encouraging light. Remember, though, that the statement that you've created and are enthused about may represent a significant change of direction to your audience. The change may be unsettling, or even threatening, to them in some ways. Your new direction for the future is usually altering the status quo. The best approach is to let them know that you've given serious thought to your future ambition and you want to share it with them. Tell them to listen carefully and not react until you have fully developed the possibilities that you see ensuing from your Focused Intent with them.

"If you think you can do a thing or think you can't do a thing, you're right."
—Henry Ford, Industrialist

Your clarity, conviction, and patience will help you gain the encouragement of others. In some cases, you may discover unexpected expressions of support in others joining you to fulfill your Focused Intent. We will dedicate several steps in the process to building a *Network of Assistance* in Chapters 7, 9, and 10 as critical components of your High-Performance Operating System.

4.4 "What" before "how"

I have often noticed that when I'm in the role of manager, friend, or parent, my initial response can appear critical to the aspirations of those seeking my approval. If I ask people too early in their process of formulation "How are you going to do that?" I may well drive them backward in their initial enthusiasm. This question can be received as too critical, or worse, it could be asked at a point in their thinking that would cause them to rely on past experiences or insufficient planning. A more supportive question at that point would be "Have you thought what the next steps might be to achieve your intent?"

By design, your Focused Intent is a statement that covers the "what" and its impact. It doesn't describe "how" you will accomplish it. It is important to maintain the distinction between what objectives you've set and how you and others will work toward the completion of those ends. This separation between results and activities is a key feature in sustaining your High-Performance Operating System.

In contrast, the logic of your default operating system has "what" and "how" collapsed in a self-limiting cycle. In this flawed reasoning, the reference point for what can happen is currently based on what has previously occurred. If you could only move ahead on your passions and commitments by using your current knowledge of how to do so, you would be tethered by the limits of your history. You would be damned to repeat what is in your experience rather than be open to new learning and resources that is prompted by the necessity to achieve new objectives in a new way. The ability to develop innovative approaches and solutions is the foundation of progress.

The logic of your default operating system has "what" and "how" collapsed in a self-limiting cycle.

A defining characteristic of the High-Performance Operating System is your ability to envision a possibility and commit to its fulfillment before you necessarily have the experience, resources, or know-how to achieve it. This is the engine of entrepreneurship.

All the great success stories from Silicon Valley, as well as countless other inspiring accounts of achievement, are founded on the principle of confronting the doubts of uncertainty, credibility, and experience.

In my work with the venture capital community, I am called on to assess investment opportunities, especially with early-stage start-up companies. I look at three basic aspects in judging the soundness of underwriting a new venture's business plan:

- The quality of the management team
- The product or service
- The market or potential scale of demand

The ability to predict the success of a company is predominantly a function of the quality of the team. Although some skills of analysis and divination are required to validate market assumptions and product credibility, the character of the team speaks the loudest.

Conservative logic will examine the relevant experience of team members. However, the savviest and most successful investors will bet on the ability of the leaders to respond creatively and courageously to the infinite number of unknown factors that the team must confront and overcome in the course of bringing home a success.

Large segments of conventional wisdom are built on the established mandate of "Learn, practice, and achieve." I have no argument with the soundness of these commandments as applied to known avenues of accomplishment. However, our ability to take risks, to demonstrate valor in the face of known and unknown barriers, is essential for transcending the gravitational field of our pasts.

It is perfectly acceptable at this phase in the deployment of your statement of Focused Intent to respond to the question "How are you going to do that?" as follows: "I don't know. I will get back to you in a week with an initial plan."

 High-Performance Operating System—Cornerstone 2

> **Envision a possibility and commit to its fulfillment before you necessarily have the experience, resources, or know-how to achieve it.**

If you know exactly what's required and how you will fulfill your Focused Intent, you have probably aimed too low or settled on a predictable goal. Not entirely knowing how to proceed to achieve an exciting outcome is, at least for now, exactly where you want to be. Stay tuned.

STORE IN MEMORY

- Your Focused Intent states what you will achieve and its desired impact. It is your intention succinctly stated at a strategic level.

- What will assist you is "not knowing" how you will realize your Focused Intent. Make sure the scope or importance of your Focused Intent ensures you break from immediately comforting solutions.

- You can fulfill your Focused Intent by dividing your world into the highest-level Pathways of Action to be managed.

- We are approaching the sharp corner in your process where "What?"and "How?" intersect with "Who?" Once you, or another person you enlist, have ownership of an outcome and something's at stake, you see the game and the field of play quite differently.

- Your ability to focus and to build on your core enthusiasm, knowing you will somehow succeed, is your platform for enlisting the support of others.

- Responsibility in the High-Performance Operating System is a choice that you freely make as a capable being. Declaring what you are willing to be responsible for shows where you stand and what you stand for.

- At the core of responsibility is a commitment to oneself. Responsibility and the commitments that flow from this way of being are forged in our ability to give and honor our word. Our word then becomes the basis of our actions in life, including at work.

- A promise is an offer to perform against specific measures: Who? What? Where? What quality? Who will be informed? These conditions are specifications for success in the High-Performance Operating System.

- You and I are more inclined to offer promises of performance when we envision an exciting and compelling possibility. Go to work on building possibilities with others.

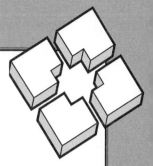

CHAPTER 5.0

Fire Alarm!

Revealing issues and concerns

"For a long time, it had seemed to me that life was about to begin—real life. But there was always some obstacle in the way. Something to be got through first, some unfinished business, time still to be served, a debt to be paid. Then life would begin. At last it dawned on me that these obstacles *were* my life.

—ALFRED D'SOUZA, THEOLOGIAN

 Preview

5.1 **But, what if?** The irony is the more ambitious your Focused Intent, the more potentially corrosive reservations will dominate your thoughts.

5.2 **Issues and concerns** We will use your initial expression of issues and concerns to demonstrate how you can alter the context, or frame of reference, of what you are saying in order to elicit desired responses in your audience.

5.3 **Your opening for action** Once you have examined your issues and concerns and given them appropriate expression as powerful questions, you can move to higher levels of performance in fulfilling your Focused Intent.

5.4 **The *awful truth*** These questions are designed to clear your "default memory." They are useful in accessing issues and considerations below the surface in your default operating system.

5.5 **Being *right*** The entire logic of the default operating system is a paradigm in which we react in a desperate attempt to be right in order to ensure our survival.

5.6 **Being effective** In the High-Performance Operating System, you have the opportunity to be effective. No one may notice the enormous and courageous effort you made to override your default logic and that of others.

5.7 **Hold your horses** Suggesting that someone not act too soon is rarely acceptable in the ever-increasing tempo of business and life in general.

5.1   But, what if?

The moment we commit to any grand enterprise—a new mortgage, the next job, marriage—a flood of considerations fills our thoughts.

"But, what if:

- I'm unable to make the payments?"
- my new boss doesn't like me?"
- I can't live up to her expectations?"

Left to the reactive devices of your default operating system, these considerations will undermine your Focused Intent. If not monitored and managed carefully, your self-doubt will subvert your will. Remember that within the logic of your default operating system, "What" you intend to do and "how" you must proceed to do it are collapsed together. The irony is the more ambitious your Focused Intent, the more these potentially corrosive reservations will dominate your thoughts with louder and more frequent distractions. Imagine waking at 3 a.m. to the recurring chorus of "What if?"

I propose to do something with these considerations that takes us beyond their usual distracting grasp. In most cases, the pull of your default operating system will demand that you attend to these doubts and concerns now. In this chapter, I will ask you to register them in a specific format within the storage capability of your High-Performance Operating System. We will return to them later when we've installed the *utilities* that will allow you to resolve, or process, them with greater power and efficiency.

5.2   Issues and concerns

When you think about fulfilling your Focused Intent, what considerations, issues, and concerns do you have? What are the *"yeah, buts"* in your own mind, or that might be in the mind of others, that could reduce the efficacy of your planning? Are these examples familiar to you?

- "I'm already very busy with my existing assignments."

- "We may not have the budget to achieve the move."
- "It's difficult to get people to focus and prioritize."

On *Spec Sheet 5.2a,* write the issues and concerns that come up when you think about fulfilling your Focused Intent.

SPEC SHEET 5.2A
ISSUES AND CONCERNS

In the space below, write the issues and concerns or considerations that you have when you think about achieving your Focused Intent. (Example responses are provided.)

My issues and concerns about fulfilling my *Focused Intent* are:

1. *(I may not have enough money to sustain the start up period of my own company)*

_____

_____

_____

2. *(Clients may not want to work for a new company)*

_____

_____

_____

3. *(Will I be able to attract key talent to work for me?)*

_____

_____

4. _____

_____

_____

_____

5. _____

_____

_____

_____

When you have your issues and concerns in written form, you can more easily regard them with some objective distance. Having these considerations in front of you gives you greater control of them.

You've probably stated your considerations in the manner of the examples I provided. They represent what most concerns you, expressed rationally, calmly, and professionally.

We will use your initial expression of issues and concerns to demonstrate how you can alter the context, or frame of reference, of what you are saying in order to elicit desired responses in your audience. In the following sequence of instructions, I will guide you in altering the expression of your issues and concerns but not the essence of their importance. In doing so, you will gain a measure of mastery in how you relate to your considerations.

We often talk about our concerns "professionally," or with an element of detachment, as the following example vividly demonstrates:

"Combustible material has spontaneously ignited in the corner of the room and has issued smoke and particulates into the air."

That's rather a long-winded, technical, unemotional explanation to communicate a vital concern.

Now I'll make the same point but say it in a different way, without changing the message: Fire!

Fire! I've consciously created the concern as an urgent and compelling problem. I've designed my communication to get your attention. I want to bring the issue into sharp contrast against the dulling background of "business as usual." I call this process *fire alarm!*

Let's look again at the earlier three examples of issues and concerns, now expressed as urgent problems, problems that would be of serious concern to the listener:

- "I've no time to do any additional work!"
- "We'll run out of money if we move!"
- "We don't know what to do next, and that will cost us sales and customer satisfaction!"

"Life cannot wait until the scientists have explained the universe. We cannot put off living until we are ready. The most salient characteristic of life is its coerciveness; it is always urgent, here and now, without any possible postponement. Life is fired at us point blank."

—JOSE ORTEGA Y GASSET, WRITER AND PHILOSOPHER

I'm not saying this phrasing is necessarily an accurate analysis or that it predicts the future. All I'm asking you to do at this stage is gain the skill of consciously modifying the context and mood of what you compose. Learning this skill starts to shift the way the concerns occur for you and others. However, it's not the final move of the game.

Your turn now. For practice, I ask that you to change the frame of reference of the issues and concerns that you wrote about in *Spec Sheet 5.2a* and now write them as *problems* without changing their essence or message. Reframe your considerations as problems that would "wake up" your listener and write them in *Spec Sheet 5.2b*, below. For this exercise, make them urgent, serious problems: fire alarms! Bring these urgent problems forward within your commitment to pierce through "business as usual" and stir others to act.

Referring to your issues and concerns as you've written them in **Spec Sheet 5.2a**, restate them as serious and urgent problems—*fire alarms!*

My *fire alarms!* in fulfilling my *Focused Intent* are:

1. *(I won't have enough money to sustain my start-up period)*
   _____
   _____

2. *(I will not be appealing for new clients)*
   _____
   _____

3. *(I won't be able to attract key talent to my firm)*
   _____
   _____

4. _____
   _____
   _____

5. _____
   _____
   _____

Now you've got our attention!

The third and last time we state these issues and concerns (now expressed as fire alarms), we will use a format generated from your High-Performance Operating System. This format will allow you to store these concerns as open, alive questions that will serve you to reach more complete and satisfying solutions as you develop and fulfill your Focused Intent.

This time I am asking you to convert the fire alarms into a specific form of question, questions that begin with the word "what" or "how."

For example:

- "How can I manage my time differently to allow me to pursue my Focused Intent?"
- "What ideas can we develop to increase the budget and finance the move?"
- "How can we ensure we find a focus and set priorities for sales and customer satisfaction?"

The simple device of composing a question that starts with "What" or "How" will allow you to transform your original issues and concerns into powerful open questions, without altering the essence of those considerations.

SPEC SHEET 5.2C
POWERFUL QUESTIONS

In the space provided, restate the fire alarms that you wrote above in *Spec Sheet 5.2b* as powerful questions that begin with "what" or "how."

My powerful questions about fulfilling my Focused Intent are:

1. *(How can I ensure that I have adequate funding and reserves to sustain my business start-up?)*

2. *(What is required in order to present a compelling Value Proposition to new clients?)*

_____

_____

3. *(How can I enlist key employees to join my firm?)*

_____

_____

_____

4. _____

_____

_____

5. _____

_____

_____

5.3   Your opening for action

Thanks for your persistence in working through these various ways of framing your issues. This exercise was designed to give you skills to consciously alter the context of what you say. In addition, you have altered your original issues and concerns. What's the advantage?

I most commonly hear people describe the benefits in the following ways:

- ■ "These questions cause me to think in terms of resolving the issue."
- ■ "Stated this way, the questions are action oriented."
- ■ "While composing the question, I already started to think of ideas of what to do."

- "The questions, as stated, don't suggest that someone is to blame for the issues or problems."
- "No one needs to be defensive about the past."

Remember, the "what" and "how" format is quite specific, as it produces open-ended questions. They cause you and your audience to view the issues in a new, more thoughtful light and to develop fresh ideas in a spirit of resolution.

Let's look a little closer at other forms of questioning. You will get a very different equation if you ask closed questions that demand a "yes/no" response:

- "Can you?"
- "Do we?"
- "Is it likely that?"

"Why" questions, such as the following, will produce another form of verbal math altogether:

- "Why can't we?"
- "Why do you say that?"
- "Why didn't it happen?"

"Why" questions will usually generate a "because" from your responder. The "because" is almost always unhelpful in discovering the real source of the issue. For example, a situation commonly experienced in business meetings and born of the default operating system goes like this:

A member of the team walks into the 8 a.m. staff meeting at 8:14 a.m. The boss says (or at least thinks what's on everyone's mind), "Why are you late?"

The team member now has to come up with an acceptable reason for being late. "I got stuck in traffic" usually has the greatest currency.

Of course, "I was stuck in traffic" didn't really cause the worker's lateness. Yes, the traffic was probably heavy. However, the employee is grasping the most obvious and marketable excuse. If this team member knew he would receive a $10,000 bonus for arriving on time, a different outcome most assuredly would have resulted. "Traffic" would have been dealt with differently.

Actually, the boss is more interested in a response to the question "What do you have to manage so you will be on time to future staff meetings?" This question asks the team member to be responsible for his prompt attendance, beyond the pale of convenient and commonly accepted excuses.

I am not saying you must never ask the question "Why?" I am saying don't ask "Why?" when you actually are wanting to discover "What happened?" and "What can you or we do differently in future?"

Once you have examined your issues and concerns and given them appropriate expression as *powerful questions*, you can move to higher levels of performance in fulfilling your Focused Intent.

5.4   The *awful truth*

There is a deeper examination of issues and concerns that reside below the surface of social convention that is often required to move forward with energy. The *awful truth* is what you say that clears the air and releases you and others to relate and act with a new sense of freedom. This includes the permission you cede to yourself to fully communicate your considerations.

The following questions are designed to clear your *default memory*. They are useful in accessing issues and considerations below the surface in your default operating system. Once you can tell the truth to yourself about these embedded concerns, you have a new relationship to these unexpressed issues that frees your self-expression and the conditions that support your success.

Please respond to the following questions if you think they are relevant to your working life. If a particular question does not prompt a response, or raise an issue, move on to the next question. (Example responses are provided.)

What have you been saying that "hasn't been heard"? (You said it, but your listener didn't seem to acknowledge or act on it.)

(I was told my budget was going to be approved, but no word of its status was ever communicated)

What have you been thinking and not saying?

(Our processes for satisfying the customer are not being followed by some of my peers)

What "can't" you say? (If you were to say it, your listener "couldn't take it" or you couldn't bear to say it)

(I can't say that product doesn't work as advertised)

What's the awful truth about your company?

(Our company is living off of its past reputation)

What's the awful truth about your department, or team?

(My team covers over discord with inappropriate humor)

What's the awful truth about some of your personal relationships? (Be specific to individuals.)

(My relationship with John is always based on competing for the boss's favor)

What's the awful truth about you?

(I haven't been working up to my fullest potential, and I blame my performance on external factors)

You may be more comfortable responding silently to some of these questions if you don't want to commit your answers to paper. The valuable part of the exercise is first telling the awful truth to yourself. Then see whether you are willing to communicate to others, in a setting that is appropriate and safe.

You demonstrate courage when you communicate fully and completely. It is an essential action in achieving your Focused Intent.

You demonstrate courage when you communicate fully and completely. It is an essential action in achieving your Focused Intent. "Big" people, those who are up to big achievements in their lives, are usually willing to share their honest responses to the above questions with others. All parties report a sense of relief at communicating the unsaid, which most other people sensed anyway. The mood always shifts when you tell the truth about what's happening: you and others can take it and move forward in a new clearing for accomplishment.

5.5   Being *right*

Display 5.5 (opposite) reveals the architecture of the default operating system and the High-Performance Operating System.

I will walk you through the core logic of the two systems illustrated in this model and how you navigate, in practical terms, from one

Display 5.5   Default and High-Performance systems

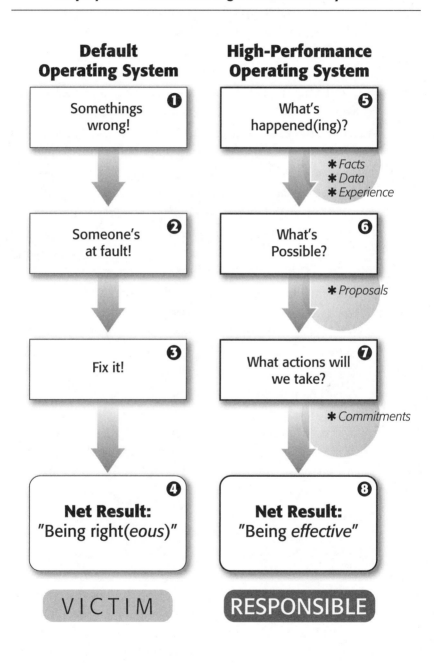

Default Operating System

High-Performance Operating System

1 Somethings wrong!

5 What's happened(ing)?

* Facts
* Data
* Experience

2 Someone's at fault!

6 What's Possible?

* Proposals

3 Fix it!

7 What actions will we take?

* Commitments

4 **Net Result:** "Being right(*eous*)"

8 **Net Result:** "Being *effective*"

VICTIM

RESPONSIBLE

system to the other. At first, the core logic of the default system may seem controversial. I recommend, though, that you read the complete description with an open mind before you react to or reject the picture I am painting.

Let's start by examining the flow of the model as it moves vertically through each step. I'll begin by looking at the Default Operating System as it's depicted in the left column in *Display 5.5*. I will use the bracketed numbers on the display to refer to the three elements of the comparison.

The core logic of the Default Operating System was installed early in our lives. Actually, it precedes us, individually. We didn't invent it. We arrived at the "party" well after it started. Let's say someone handed us a "drink" as we entered.

The name of this metaphoric "drink" is "Something's wrong!" (reference **#1**). This in itself isn't bad or wrong. It's just the way the core logic of the default operating system is organized. The coded logic of the default operating system is designed to ensure our survival. More precisely, it is designed to maintain the continuity of who we believe ourselves to be, our identity, if you will.

This logic applies to virtually everything that happens in our environment. As unknown events occur around us, they are perceived as a change of stasis by our default operating system. Remember the logic: change is a potential threat. The default logic serves a most practical requirement. It keeps us from putting our hand on the hot stove or from driving into the oncoming lanes of traffic. "Something's wrong!"

In the automatic logic of the default operating system, another thought is triggered almost simultaneously with "Something's wrong!": "Someone's at fault" (reference **#2**). The logic goes: if something's wrong, then someone's at fault. It must be him, or her, or them, or it. "Someone's at fault."

This system of logic may not appeal to our higher sense of ourselves. It certainly isn't very complimentary. However, map it honestly against your everyday experiences. Test it in your private thoughts and reactions. "Something's wrong; someone's at fault." Pick up today's newspaper, and look at the headlines. The silent logic assembles our perceptions: "Something's wrong; someone's at fault."

Sales blames manufacturing. Marketing blames engineering. The unions blame management. The Hatfields blame the McCoys.

Our explanations and justifications of our own behavior and work product are calculated to ensure that we survive any accusation of fault.

One pleasant exception to the rule of this default logic is how it applies to ourselves. Our public presentation is designed to ensure that if someone's at fault, it isn't us. Our explanations and justifications of our own behavior and work product are calculated to ensure that we survive any accusation of fault. The logic of the default operating system is infallible.

The final step in the format of the default logic is to "Fix it!" (reference #3). Soldier on against the undertow of an unrelenting cycle. You may actually produce incremental results. The operating instruction is "Fix it!" and futilely attempt to derive satisfaction in the process.

The entire logic of the default operating system is a paradigm, or unobserved pattern of belief. In this paradigm, we exist in almost total reaction to our environment. We operate in a system of reaction to the circumstances. "It" determines us.

What's the net result for us as determined by the logic of the default operating system? What's the payoff? Simply stated, we get to experience "Being *right*" (reference #4). This is the practical, moment-to-moment output of the default logic. Survival of our identity translates to "being right" in everyday behavior. I didn't say accurate. I mean "right" as in self-righteous. Usually, the default logic has our being right at the expense of someone or something being wrong.

Expressions of the default operating system logic being right include:

- Blaming others
- Finding fault
- Resisting what's apparent
- Being a *victim*

I have never walked away from a heated argument where, in my self-referential logic, I didn't win. I showed them. They were wrong, and I proved it to myself as I incessantly replayed the debate in my head.

5.6   Being effective

Yes, you have an alternative to the tenacious logic of the default operating system. The protocol to override the stubborn grasp of the default operating system is elusive, however. You have to see the default logic in operation as it exercises its influence. You have to observe yourself caught in the act of being right or making others wrong. What makes this monitoring so tricky is how commonplace, and therefore invisible, the behavior can be.

A victim doesn't have to be responsible for anything.

As you consider the expressions of being right, the logic may appear convoluted. How can a victim be right? Well, you can't get more right or self-*right*eous than being a victim. A victim doesn't have to be responsible for anything. The more you see yourself as a victim, the more you can blame someone or something else and make that person or thing wrong. Sadly, we have elevated being a victim to a high art form in our culture.

Most people may not be able to see themselves in the blind trap of the default logic, but they sure know other people who fit the description perfectly. The logic explains so much about them. But the more we insist that we aren't like that, the more we are playing out the logic. The ultimate example, self-proclaimed enlightenment, "I have risen above it all," is simply another slippery trap of the default operating system.

Now let's work through the logic of the High-Performance Operating System, as shown in the right-hand column in *Display 5.5*. You can access your High-Performance Operating System through two steps:

- Observe the default logic occurring.
- Choose to act from the alternative logic (which follows) of the High-Performance Operating System.

Both the logic of the default operating system and that of the High-Performance Operating System are activated by an event we experience and reactions we have:

■ In the default operating system, we interpret the event as threatening, and our reaction is "Something's wrong!"
■ In the High-Performance Operating System, we see the same event, and our reaction is a question: "What happened?"

Three powerful questions, operating in sequence, drive the logic of the High-Performance Operating System.

1. "What happened?" (reference **#5**)
2. "What's possible?" (reference **#6**)
3. "What action will we take?" (reference **#7**)

The first question, "What happened?" (or "What's happening?"), is calculated to call forward *facts*, *data*, and the *current situation*. All thoughtful investigation starts at this stage: What actually happened separate from our interpretation or emotion? Here are the specific questions that yield "What happened?"

■ "What are the facts?"
■ "What data do we have?"
■ "What is the current situation?"

Once you have determined what's actually happening, you ask the second question, "What's possible?" This question acts as the engine for creating new futures. You and others respond to it with ideas and new approaches to consider and clarify. You build a field of possibilities from which to determine the best actions. What's possible?

In the third step in the high-performance logic sequence, you ask, "What action will we take?" At this point, what could be becomes what will be.

■ "What action will we take?"
■ "What will we enact?"
■ "What will we commit to?"

We experience the birth of our commitment to act. Our "perform-ance" hits the ground running in the form of actions we declare from resolving these questions.

In most organizations, and to many people in everyday situations, "commitment" is often a word and an action to avoid. In the default logic that operates in these situations, "commitment" is equated with obligation, burden, or fear associated with being blamed if something expected doesn't occur. In your high-performance logic, "commitment" is a term of choice designed to empower you and the steps required for success.

"The price of greatness is responsibility."
—WINSTON CHURCHILL, BRITISH PRIME MINISTER

The specific expressions of "commitment" as actions in language are *promises* and *requests*. Promises and requests are the basic building blocks of your High-Performance Operating System, the equivalent of the 1s and 0s at the core of a computer's coded soul. I will cover the practical applications of commitment in greater detail in Chapter 8.

When you locate yourself in the *alternative logic* of the High-Performance Operating System, you are at the center of a system of creation. What you and others create are commitments: your com-mitment to act and the committed actions of others. The net result? You get to be *effective*.

You experience a new relationship to the circumstances in your life and no longer view yourself as a victim of those circumstances.

Now here's something to keep in mind. I've worked with this system for more than 25 years, and I haven't yet found a way to be both right and effec-tive at the same time. In order to be effective, you have to give up being right. That's the sum of the math. For many people, for much of the time, being right matters more than being effective in producing breakthroughs. They would rather be dead right. In the High-Performance Operating System, you only get to be effective. And no one may notice the enormous and courageous effort you made to override your default logic and that of others.

You have a choice. At any moment, you can choose to be right or to be effective. To act as a victim is to seek the agreement of others that "Something's wrong" and "Someone's to blame." The alternative is to be *responsible* to discover "What happened" and "What's possible."

> "People are always blaming their circumstances for what they are. I don't believe in circumstances. The people who get on in this world are the people who get up and look for the circumstances they want, and if they can't find them, make them."
> —GEORGE BERNARD SHAW, PLAYWRIGHT

The kind of responsibility that you install through your High-Performance Operating System is not an exercise in fault or blame. It goes beyond right and wrong, allowing you to see cause and effect in a system of logic beyond the limits of the default operating system. Your willingness to be responsible represents a stand you take to achieve something great in your life. From that stand, you experience a new relationship to the circumstances in your life and no longer view yourself as a victim of those conditions.

Your Focused Intent and your stand to achieve it constitute a *platform* from which to observe these logic systems at work. You are now equipped to make powerful choices by virtue of the commitments you've made. "What" and "how" become the questions that move you from a reactive condition that determines you to a creative realm where you are the author of your experience.

5.7   Hold your horses

We will return to the questions you have registered here in Chapter 8. For now, I ask that you leave them as open questions. See whether you can resist the temptation of acting too soon. I know that suggesting that someone not act is rarely acceptable in the ever-increasing tempo of business and life in general.

Here's the offer on the table: when you resolve the questions you have formulated in the course of working though my process, you will have the tools to take more effective and inspired actions. As you proceed, you will continue to gain momentum and confidence to bring effective action to your Focused Intent.

STORE IN MEMORY

⌘ The moment we commit to any grand enterprise—a new mortgage, the next job, marriage—a flood of considerations fills our thoughts. "But, what if?"

⌘ What are the "yeah, buts" in your own mind, or that you think might be in the mind of others, that could interfere with your planning?

⌘ The "what" and "how" format produces open-ended questions. They cause you and your audience to view the issues in a new, more thoughtful light and to develop fresh ideas in a spirit of resolution.

⌘ The awful truth is what you say that clears the air and releases you and others to relate and act with a new sense of freedom. This includes the permission you cede to yourself to fully communicate your considerations.

⌘ The core logic of the default operating system was installed early in our lives. Actually, it precedes us, individually. We didn't invent it.

⌘ Change is a potential threat. The default logic serves a most practical requirement. It is designed to ensure our survival.

⌘ Three powerful questions, operating in sequence, drive the logic of the High-Performance Operating System. These questions drive toward new commitments from the observation that "something happened" and "something's possible."

⌘ You have a choice. At any moment, you can choose to be right or to be effective.

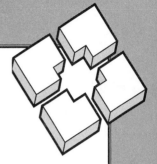

CHAPTER 6.0

From *What* to *How*
Constructing *pathways for action*

"Strategy without tactics is the slowest route to victory. Tactics without strategy is the noise before defeat."

—SUN TZU, MILITARY STRATEGIST

 Preview

6.1 **Navigate the unknown** You will navigate in new territory with clarity, rigor, and discipline to attain your goals. Guided steps will aid you in constructing a strategic display that will allow you and others to work from the same page.

6.2 *Pathways for Action* Imagine you are the senior commander of a military campaign; you initially organize your efforts at the highest, most efficient levels in order to accomplish your stated aims.

6.3 **Nothing great is created alone** Things become real when someone actually has to take action; someone will have to take ownership of each of the strategic Pathways for Action you have identified.

6.4 **The freedom of *responsibility*** In our default operating system, responsibility equates with obligation, burden, blame, and liability. No wonder countless organizations and relationships avoid it like a rabid squirrel.

6.5 **The choice of *accountability*** A specific form of commitment, accountability has both organizational and personal dimensions. You and I can't make someone accountable. It is an explicit expression of choice.

6.6 **The *Who*** Select people who can best support your efforts to fulfill your Focused Intent in the strategic pathways you have created.

6.1   Navigate the unknown

Your Focused Intent states what you will achieve and its desired impact. It is your intention succinctly stated at a strategic level. The origins of strategy will be a useful reference when I ask you in this chapter to plan the fulfillment of your Focused Intent. Strategy originated as the science and art of military command. Referencing these military precedents will be informative as you navigate *Pathways for Action* with clarity, rigor, and discipline to attain your goals. I have designed steps in this chapter to aid you in constructing a strategic display that will allow you and others who will come to support you to work from the "same page."

"I think most of us are looking for a calling, not a job. Most of us, like the assembly line worker, have jobs that are too small for our spirit. Jobs are not big enough for people."
—STUDS TERKEL, BROADCASTER AND AUTHOR

What will also assist you at this stage in your progression through my process is "not knowing" how you will realize your Focused Intent. If you can simply jot down a "to-do" list or apply your familiar off-the-shelf routines to reach your Focused Intent, the objective you've chosen is probably too predictable. Make sure the scope or importance of your Focused Intent ensures that you break from those immediately comforting solutions.

Proceed by questioning what you believe you already know. Your undaunted commitment to fulfill your intent, framed in the continued inquiry "What's possible?" will provide the ticket you're seeking.

6.2   Pathways for Action

In order to proceed beyond your Focused Intent (the what) to the next level of planning, we are going to construct Pathways for Action (the how). These *pathways* are the next level of development of a plan that will provide clarity and direction as you move forward.

Spec Sheet 6.2a (opposite) is a template on which you can draft a navigational matrix that will have all the elements necessary to transition from "what" to "how."

Write your Focused Intent in the center of the illustrated circle now.

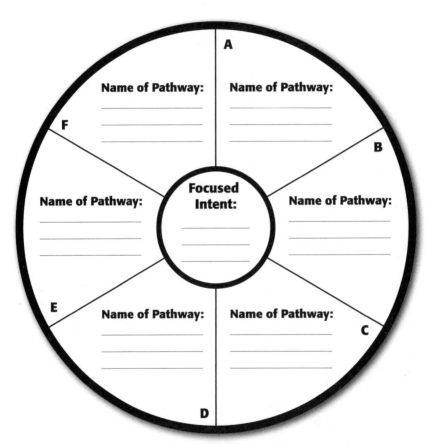

Each segment is assigned to a pilot & co-pilot:

Name of Pathway	Pilot (name)	Co-Pilot (name)
A		
B		
C		
D		
E		
F		

These elements are represented in the diagram as:

1. Focused Intent (target)
2. Name of pathway
3. Pilot/co-pilot

In the center circle (target), write your Focused Intent. If your intent is lengthy, you can abbreviate it in a phrase. For example, if your intent is "I will open my own business within one year so that I achieve my dream of independence and prosperity," a symbolic phrase to represent it could be "My Shop!" or "The Dream Fulfilled." Don't labor too long on this; the goal here is to have a target that you and others can relate to easily.

This focused target will serve as the navigation point toward which, in your next planning step, your Pathways for Action, will converge.

You will use the segments in the next layer of the circle to establish the strategic Pathways for Action that will guide the planning toward your intent. I have initially divided the circle into six segments, represented by the dotted lines. You may end up with five or even seven pathways, but most teams seem to settle on six without prompting. You can arrive at any number of segments that are appropriate for your Focused Intent. If you have additional pathways, just add dotted lines to the existing six segments of the circle to form additional divisions.

Let's use a military example to give you an idea of how to determine pathways that are appropriate to your Focused Intent. In 1991, Operation Desert Storm was established around a strategic Focused Intent, stated as the liberation of Kuwait from Iraqi forces. Imagine you were the senior commander of that campaign; you would have initially organized your efforts at the highest levels to ensure the most efficient management of resource requirements. In order to accomplish your stated aim, you would have determined the strategic Pathways for Action that you would directly manage. In this case, you would direct your assets through division of labor seen at the most senior level of planning. Here's a representative list:

- Land forces
- Air forces
- Naval forces
- Intelligence services
- Logistics
- Diplomatic relations

You would likely have thousands of details to manage. You would access this seemingly unmanageable number of tasks through an efficiently organized set of pathways. The senior members of staff you would call to your planning sessions represent these pathways, one person for each of the strategic pathways.

You can fulfill your Focused Intent in similar ways. You begin by dividing your world into the highest-level Pathways of Action to be managed. Whether you work alone or have access to unlimited resources, you would organize your efforts by determining the most senior categories where action and results are required. How would you organize your effort?

Maybe you can approach your Focused Intent by developing Pathways for Action along traditional organizational divisions:

Pathway	Action
Finance	Acquiring and managing the required funds
Marketing	Presenting your effort in the optimum light
Training	Learning new skills or gaining experience
Process development	Developing how you would operate in a given area
Product	Perfecting what you are envisioning or providing
Alliances	Attracting key players with whom to partner
Sales	Selling the idea or service to target users

You are not asking yourself who would do this work or what immediate tasks are required. You are asking what pathways, or categories of action, you would organize to fulfill the Focused Intent. Write them down initially in *Spec Sheet 6.2b* (below). You are not limited for now to any specific number of pathways. Instead, concentrate on capturing what calls for managing at a strategic level. If you are working in concert with others, ask for their input.

SPEC SHEET 6.2B
STRATEGIC PATHWAYS (WORKSHEET)

In the following space, write your initial thoughts for the Pathways for Action that will deliver your Focused Intent. When you have settled on the final list of Pathways for Action, transfer the names of the pathways to *Spec Sheet 6.2a*: (Example responses are provided.)

A. *(Sales)* _____

_____

_____

B. *(Recruitment)* _____

_____

_____

C. *(Funding/finance)* _____

_____

_____

D. *(Operations)* _____

_____

_____

E. *(Product development)*

_____

_____

_____

F. *(Research)*

_____

_____

_____

If you have fewer than six pathways, make sure you've covered all the domains where you require results. If you have more than six pathways, my bet is that some will logically "nest" within higher-order pathways as you work through your list.

For example, if you are analyzing the requirements for a military campaign such as Operation Desert Storm, you might have listed armor, infantry, and training. In our model, you could logically put armor and infantry under land forces. You could put training as a new separate category, or you could place it as a lower-order element for both naval and land forces to manage, as *Display 6.2c* (following page) shows. It's your call.

- ■ Naval forces
  - • Training
- ■ Land forces
  - • Training
  - • Armor
  - • Infantry

We're working toward generating necessary and sufficient strategic pathways. When you have arrived at the number of pathways you are satisfied with, put the name of each pathway in the pie-shaped segments in *Display 6.2a*. We will account for the lower-order elements later in my process through aspects of project management.

Display 6.2c   Example of *Pathways of Action*: Desert Storm

6.3   Nothing great is created alone

Everything becomes real when someone actually has to take action. We are approaching the sharp corner in your process where "What?" and "How" intersect with "Who?" Once you or another person you enlist have ownership of an outcome and something's at stake, you see the game and the field of play quite differently.

You may be working through this process as a sole proprietor of a business or as a manager of a team of many people. In all cases, someone will have to be responsible for, or "own," each of the strategic Pathways for Action you have identified.

If you have authored your Focused Intent as a seemingly private endeavor, you may have to own most, if not all, of the pathways. At times in my consulting practice I work on the formation of a company.

In these instances, I counsel the founder to envision the company as if it already did $30 million worth of business annually and had 100 employees. At this early stage of the venture, I ask questions to encourage the founder to think in a much larger framework:

- "What strategic pathways are required?"
- "What would the organization look like once the company is operating at full capacity?"
- "What roles are required?"

Similarly, I ask that you assume this perspective for what you intend to accomplish in moving through your process in *Choose What Works*.

From day one, this founder is thinking through a frame of reference of $30 million annually and 100 people. Although he may initially manage most of the functions, including sales, planning, and finance, he is clear what "hat" he is wearing in those roles. In each role, he has a specific plan for advancing activities toward the target. My coaching also encourages the founder to give a share of his roles to others, who could include advisors, volunteers, and friends. The founder can employ the distinctions of a High-Performance Operating System in his thinking, independent of the size or age of the business.

People often think, "If I had the resources of Bill Gates of Microsoft, Steve Jobs of Apple, or Oprah Winfrey of Harpo, I could do what they do." It's not as simple as that. I have worked with dozens of leaders and entertainers who've reached high levels of accomplishment. In most cases, these people planned and took action as though they were already successful. They were able to work in a future they envisioned and make choices and take action consistent with that achievement. They were up to something important, and they were able to inspire and attract others to join them in building it. Resources alone won't do it. Your ability to focus and to build on your core enthusiasm, knowing you will somehow succeed, is your platform for enlisting the support of others.

Let's return to the development of your navigational matrix on *Spec Sheet 6.2a*. For each of the Pathways for Action you've identified, nominate someone who can be the primary "owner" of that segment in the circle. We'll call this person the pathway "pilot." In addition, I will ask you to think about a "co-pilot" for each of these segmented pathways.

After you do that, in the next section of this chapter, I will define the accompanying responsibilities and accountabilities. These terms are often confused in the default operating system. They are both forms of commitment, which we see at play in every organization and family arrangement. Your clarity of these distinct types of commitment is essential in order to work from your High-Performance Operating System.

6.4   The freedom of *responsibility*

As I have stated previously, in our default operating system, responsibility, as an expression of commitment, is equivalent to obligation, burden, blame, and liability. No wonder countless organizations and relationships avoid it like a rabid squirrel. For many people, "It's not my fault" means "I wasn't responsible" for something that went wrong. *Responsibility* doesn't equal credit, praise, or honor, either. These attributes are simply the positive pole in the same default paradigm. They reflect evaluations and judgments in the default system of right/wrong, good/bad, or approval/disapproval.

Responsibility starts with a willingness to consider a new relationship with the circumstances in your life.

In the expanded frame of the High-Performance Operating System, responsibility starts with a willingness to consider a new relationship with the circumstances in your life. In *Display 6.4* (opposite), I have displayed this idea in *bytes*.

I can't make someone be responsible. Neither can you. No person can make someone else be responsible. It is not an assignment or title. In the default operating system, we have expectations of each other. These expectations are seldom communicated openly and explicitly, much less

Display 6.4a Categories of Commitment: *Responsibility*

Responsibility

- A commitment that you make where you don't necessarily, "own" the means to fulfill.

- *A willingness*
      to consider
          a new relationship
              with the circumstances.

(This requires going beyond "finding fault.")

agreed to. We then proceed in the default operating system to hold others hostage to expectations they never agreed to. Welcome to "us" and "them."

Responsibility in the High-Performance Operating System is a choice that you freely make as a capable being. Declaring what you are willing to be responsible for shows where you stand and what you stand for. Responsibility is caused by your speaking and carried by the authority of your word.

Responsibility begins with the willingness and the openness to see a situation differently. This willingness to see beyond the obvious is related to the commitments you have made, the person you have set yourself to be. In this process of building your "response ability," you examine your identity, the person you hold yourself to be, and what you can become. Mother, father, partner, manager, and friend are all roles that can strengthen your identity and freedom to be responsible.

To bring this point home to the groups I work with, I ask a volunteer to answer some simple personal questions in the group setting. The dialogue usually goes like this:

"Are you married?"

"Yes."

"Do you have children?"

"Yes."

"In your relationship with your spouse, what 'percentage' are you responsible for your kids?" (I let them know it's a trick question, one that demands a response beyond "50%.")

"Um, 100%?"

"Bingo!"

Whether married or not, members of the group to whom I'm speaking connect with this vivid example. People see that in this instance, their relationship to their kids goes beyond the current circumstances. They have declared that they are responsible for the welfare of their children. Period. It is their stand toward their children, solely because they say so. Their *declaration* does not depend on whether their marriage continues or whether they live with their children or even what the law states. This responsibility can even extend beyond their lifespan through the extension of wills and insurance.

At the core of responsibility is a commitment to oneself.

Although this kind of relationship to one's family could be termed "natural," it is not a product of biology. What appears to be a commitment to children is upon deeper examination a relationship to our declared values, to the dignity of our lives. At the core of responsibility is a commitment to oneself. Responsibility and the commitments that flow from this way of being are forged in our ability to give and honor our word. Our word then becomes the basis of our actions in life, including at work.

Responsibility generated in the High-Performance Operating System can apply to professional as well as personal circumstances. In an organizational setting, you can define and apply responsibility arising from the High-Performance Operating System quite practically. Responsibility at work is a commitment you make where you don't necessarily have or control the resources to fulfill it. Enacting your responsibility toward these seemingly uncontrollable commitments requires your ability to perform confidently in the face of a paradox: How can I *promise* what I don't control? Now the game becomes more interesting.

Business is increasingly conducted in a matrix of projects. Traditional lines of authority are blurred; functional boundaries are malleable. Responsibility in this environment calls for us to be effective in a field of interdependent relationships. This level of responsibility necessitates that we understand and design our actions from the big picture. It requires us to present compelling ideas and plans that move others to act. Our ability to influence others has replaced entitlements, demands, and coercion. Real power, in business and our relationships, is the ability to effect desired change without resorting to the application of force, authority, or threat.

"A hero is someone who understands the responsibility that comes with his freedom."

—BOB DYLAN, SINGER AND SONGWRITER

Your declaration of responsibility and its influence on others you live and work with will alter the weight of circumstance that currently defines your success and satisfaction. Most of the limitations in our lives are determined by our perception of the gravity of circumstances. These external factors form the "because" of our existence, the explanations that we use and often believe that describe the way our lives are. Being responsible entails looking at these same conditions and asking ourselves:

- "How might this situation be different?"
- "What choices did I make that contributed to my current situation?"
- "What could I do or have done that would result in a different outcome?"
- "What have I been justifying or arguing against?"

These questions and your responses to them start to shift your relationship to being the cause rather than the effect of the conditions in your life. Telling the truth to yourself and accepting how you've "wired" situations begins to transform your relationship to "the way things are." You will experience a new freedom from cause and effect.

There are numerous examples of people who have risen above the clasp of circumstances to live and function within the scope of responsibility they have declared. Christopher Reeve, the actor who portrayed Superman, was paralyzed in a tragic horse-jumping accident. He has repurposed his life to influence a cure for spinal cord injuries. His stated intention is to walk again.

6.5   The choice of *accountability*

Accountability is a more specific form of commitment. It has both organizational and personal dimensions. Again, you and I can't make someone accountable. It is an explicit expression of choice.

Let's look more carefully at each component of the definition of accountability in *Display 6.5*.

A promise is a commitment to have your actions conform to your word. A promise is given in order to cause something to happen that won't happen just through the passing of time. For example, you don't have to promise to wake up tomorrow; your biological impulses will handle that. You may, however, have to promise to get up at 4:30 a.m. to catch a flight.

A promise is not a guarantee. A guarantee implies that if what is offered doesn't happen, compensation will be provided. People will

Display 6.5   Categories of Commitment: *Accountability*

Accountability

- A commitment that you make where you "own" the means to fulfill.

- *A promise*
     to perform
          as agreed.

generally lower the standards of performance if they will incur a penalty for not delivering as specified. Stipulating penalties is one sure way in an organization to lower performance. If you make people guarantee results, they will become risk averse, offer feeble objectives, and avoid commitment. Acknowledging and rewarding promises fulfilled is the desired alternative to produce high performance.

A promise is an offer to perform against specific measures: Who? What? Where? What quality? Who will be informed? I call these setting these conditions *specifications for success* in the High-Performance Operating System.

A promise is an offer to act within a specific period. Commitments without a "by when" are simply *good ideas*. "We'll improve sales" is one way to manage business. "We'll raise sales 10% by March 31" is another. Which do you think will cause the desired performance improvements?

A promise requires someone to listen with a sense that the possibility of achieving the promise is credible. In this sense, the person listening to the promise has an investment in the outcome. Having an audience that is committed to your achievement gives a promise real energy. The more public your promises, the more power they will have.

For example, tell yourself, silently, that you are going to lose 10 pounds and exercise every morning. You may carry out your promise, but chances are it will recede with the tide of other fleeting interests that pass through your thoughts. It falls into the category of a "New Year's resolution," a weak promise without the requisite investment of support and encouragement from others. Instead, announce to all the employees of your company in a general assembly that you are going to exercise every day. Say you will donate $10 to a favorite charity for every pound that you shake off. Ask for their support in attaining your goal. See what happens.

Only two possible outcomes stem from your promise. Either you will accomplish what you said or you won't. You are not a better person if you fulfill your promise, and you are not a bad person if you didn't meet it. Remember that promises are not predictions. They are not safe bets. In fact, if you accomplish all your promises, you are probably playing too small. If you fall short of your promises occasionally, yet you gave of yourself fully, you will develop muscles for achievement. Promising empowers you in the face of a challenge you care about. Go for it!

In an organization, people who regularly keep their promises are rewarded in a unique fashion. They are given more responsibility. In contrast, people who are known not to keep their word are banished to a horrible existence. They are listened to as if what they say doesn't matter—until they eventually depart. Some traditional companies have a particularly painful form of exile. The person is given a desk in the corner and a newspaper.

My next statement may at first appear contradictory: You can't technically promise a result. We can't control the world. We can, however, promise that our actions will be consistent with the intended result. We can respond to contingencies that arise while we are working toward the final outcome. Executed with full commitment, integrity, and urgency, our actions will take us beyond where we have historically been thwarted.

Others don't generally forget promises that you make. As good practice, proactively report on what got produced and what didn't, within your context of accountability. Such an account constitutes *closure*. It restores integrity in the system. You bring completion to the promise you've committed and to the expectations of others. You reinforce other people's regard for you and the strength of your relationship with them. People can deal with what has been completed and what hasn't; they are waiting for you to be forthcoming with an accurate and factual account.

In the default operating system, shortfalls are managed somewhat differently. I'll illustrate this point by sharing a story about a friend and his teenage son. My friend asked his son how he was going to do in math class in the upcoming semester. "I promise to get an A," the boy answered. His final grade turned out to be a C.

His son's system of default logic went like this:

Promised an A + got a C + *story* ("my teacher didn't like me") = an A.

> "The ancient Romans had a tradition: whenever one of their engineers constructed an arch, as the capstone was hoisted into place, the engineer assumed accountability for his work in the most profound way possible: he stood under the arch."
>
> —MICHAEL ARMSTRONG, CEO OF AT&T

In his mind, his intention (promise an A), plus the mark he received (C), plus his explanation (story about "teacher not liking me") equals an A. It is an airtight and closed system. It's always self-righting by virtue of his self-justifying story that is manufactured in his default logic. According to the son's default logic, the only way to improve his performance and keep his promise next term would be—you guessed it—to have a teacher who likes him. In this system of dealing with shortfalls of promises, there is no possibility of actually being accountable for his performance or self-improvement.

You and I share the same default system of logic as the hapless teenager. We've just become a bit slicker with our explanations and self-justifications.

It's a good idea, especially in business, to memorialize your accountabilities in writing. Forming a record saves a lot of grief in avoiding misunderstandings and disconnected expectations. After you meet with someone with whom you are making promises and setting accountabilities, repeat what you have agreed on, to ensure clarity. Follow up by sending a note or e-mail restating the commitments you are accountable for and your understanding of what the other person will be providing in the transaction or relationship.

You and I are more inclined to offer promises of performance when we envision an exciting and compelling possibility. Go to work on building possibilities with others. We'll talk a lot more about this in Chapter 9.0.

The example of responsibility I used earlier when I spoke about parents' relationship to their children completes the view of accountability. Those parents responded that they were 100% responsible for the welfare of their kids. Within the framework of that declaration of responsibility, they could agree on their respective accountabilities, which might be more like a 50/50 split. For example, "I'll watch the kids evenings and weekends," and "I'll care for the children on alternating weekends." These declarations demonstrate specific accountability within a broader context of responsibility. Within the shared framework of their relationship as parents, for which both partners are responsible, they are able to freely arrange practical expressions of accountability.

6.6   The *Who*

Please return to *Spec Sheet 6.2a*. Add in the names of people, in the lower table, who you feel may be able and willing to support your efforts in fulfilling your Focused Intent in the pathways of action you designated. If you are working in a team or you manage a group of people, you can assign as many "pilots" to your segments as you are comfortable with. It's also fine if you are the "pilot" in most segments and you are nominating "co-pilots" to support your efforts.

> "The first responsibility of a leader is to define reality. The last is to say 'thank you.' In between, the leader is servant."
>
> —MAX DE PREE, CEO AND AUTHOR

In the next chapter, you will learn more about how to determine what accountabilities are appropriate for pilots and co-pilots and how to have all members join you in being responsible for success.

STORE IN MEMORY

- Your Focused Intent states what you will achieve and its desired impact. It is your intention succinctly stated at a strategic level.

- What will assist you is "not knowing" how you will realize your Focused Intent. Make sure the scope or importance of your Focused Intent ensures you break from immediately comforting solutions.

- You can fulfill your Focused Intent by dividing your world into the highest-level Pathways of Action to be managed.

- We are approaching the sharp corner in your process where "What?" and "How?" intersect with "Who?" Once you, or another person you enlist, have ownership of an outcome and something's at stake, you see the game and the field of play quite differently.

- Your ability to focus and to build on your core enthusiasm, knowing you will somehow succeed, is your platform for enlisting the support of others.

- Responsibility in the High-Performance Operating System is a choice that you freely make as a capable being. Declaring what you are willing to be responsible for shows where you stand and what you stand for.

- At the core of responsibility is a commitment to oneself. Responsibility and the commitments that flow from this way of being are forged in our ability to give and honor our word. Our word then becomes the basis of our actions in life, including at work.

- A promise is an offer to perform against specific measures: Who? What? Where? What quality? Who will be informed? These conditions are specifications for success in the High-Performance Operating System.

- You and I are more inclined to offer promises of performance when we envision an exciting and compelling possibility. Go to work on building possibilities with others.

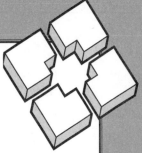

CHAPTER 7.0

Steer Toward Results
Delivering outcomes with those you depend on

"In all human affairs there are efforts, and there are results, and the strength of the effort is in the measure of the result."

—JAMES ALLEN, WRITER

 Preview

7.1   **From bored to *Board*** Your Focused Intent matters enough that you open your thinking and planning to the contributions of others. Welcome to your Strategic Board.

7.2   **We deliver** Your initial Strategic Board process is iterative; members will collaborate with you in creating, reviewing, and revising your Focused Intent.

7.3   **How come outcomes?** Your key to successful navigation of your Focused Intent is to steer toward results. Your board will keep you straight within the framework for producing results that you set up.

7.4   **Get real** Tune your High-Performance Operating System to listen for appropriate specifications for success that will underwrite the credibility of your commitments and the commitments of others.

7.5   **From dependencies to alliances** The success of almost all your results will depend on someone contributing toward the achievement of your Focused Intent. Those you depend on will gladly participate in your plans when you introduce possibilities to which they can connect.

7.1   From bored to *Board*

Your Focused Intent represents your declared future. Serving as your basis for strategy and Pathways for Action, it represents an empowering step between your history and your dreams. It is your primary reason for transformation—a big enough challenge to override default behavior and install a high-performance system in your work and life.

Your Focused Intent matters enough to open your thinking and planning to how others might contribute. Once you realize you can't or, more important, shouldn't do it alone, you step up to a new, more inclusive platform of performance.

You have nominated people as pilots and co-pilots of your Pathways for Action. Now you have an opportunity to include outside support and collaboration that will boost your achievements beyond past boundaries. Welcome to your *Strategic Board.*

A board functions in interesting and useful ways for organizations and companies:

- A board's purpose is to provide governance to management and protect the interests of stakeholders.
- The board structures accountability of the chief executive and reviews progress toward stated goals.
- The board provides perspective, experience, structure, and continuity for the public commitments of an organization.
- The board assumes responsibility for the integrity and success of the enterprise.

I have participated on more than a dozen boards. Each of these experiences was remarkable. I witnessed my self grow professionally as I served the requirements of these bodies. I realized that I had a responsibility to demonstrate the confidence and trust that came with my role. I became a bigger person in the service of a mission that was larger than me. I found my leadership "voice" when I was able to locate myself in the welfare of the entire organization. My view of responsibility expanded beyond the specific area of expertise that originally drew these organizations and companies to invite me to join their Board.

In this role on the various boards, compensation was not my primary driver. Rather, contributing to someone and something I cared about was important. One of the most productive and satisfying periods of my life was when I was extremely active in an international organization of management consultants. I received no direct payment for the leadership I provided. I had more than a full-time role in managing my own business, which had membership in this affiliation. What I contributed, though, came back to me tenfold in new learning, in an expanded sense of myself as a business leader, and in the recognition of having made a difference in the careers of others, many of whom could be viewed as competitors.

Let me share a secret with you about people. They are dying to contribute. Invite their participation, and structure a role for them in your success.

Let me share a secret with you about people. They are dying to contribute. This desire was evident to me when I watched my son, when he was two years old, pick up a hammer to help me build the deck. It is also true about your colleagues, friends, and others you admire. They want to be able to contribute to the achievement of your Focused Intent. In order to secure their contribution, you must act. Invite their participation, and structure a role for them in your success.

Convene as your Strategic Board the people you have nominated as pilots and co-pilots of your Pathways for Action. Organizing this Strategic Board is equally as relevant for you, whether your intent is a personal or professional goal. Forming, leading, and accounting to this group will be a vital aspect in achieving your Focused Intent and installing your High-Performance Operating System.

It's up to you how many people you want to bring on your board at this stage. If your Focused Intent is largely a personal achievement, you may have co-pilots to help navigate, offer perspective, and provide expertise. I recommend a minimum of three people, including you, to serve as members. If you have a more team-oriented goal, then give primary ownership to as many people as you consider realistic. Eight members are pushing the upper limits of a manageable board.

The defining characteristic of the board is that all members have both an individual accountability to work in a specific area of execution and a shared responsibility for the success of the Focused Intent.

Within each Pathway for Action represented on the board, the pilot has primary accountability to determine the outcomes required for the pathway and cause its accomplishment. The role of the co-pilot is supportive, but no less significant. Remember that the co-pilot often flies the plane. The parties involved can agree the specific responsibilities and accountabilities of these roles within each pathway.

The board and its members become a set of relationships committed to your success. It functions as a *Network of Assistance* to which your High-Performance Operating System is tuned. The quality of these linked relationships has the power to cause unprecedented and, in some cases, surprising results.

The following guidelines suggest how you can set up a Strategic Board:

- Meet individually with each person who will be a pathway pilot or co-pilot. Let them know you are up to something big in your career and in your life. Share your Focused Intent. Invite them to play a leadership role on your board in one or more of the Pathways for Action you have outlined.
- Tell each participant that in addition to having a dedicated accountability as a pilot or co-pilot, you are requesting that they participate in a board dedicated to achieving the overall Focused Intent.
- Ensure, through full discussion, that all members clearly see what they can contribute and how they will benefit from their participation. The benefit for most will be participating in something that matters. Everyone needs to be able to experience their contribution making a difference to you and others.

■ Set up a board process that doesn't require significant "overhead" in terms of time or difficulty. Let people know that you will hold periodic meetings that will be run efficiently and that their commitment of time will be respected.

■ Encourage members to participate as if the process of running the board was their "deal." They would demonstrate this level of leadership and ownership by speaking in meetings to:

   • challenge assumptions

   • demand clarity of proposals

   • call a foul ball when they see it

In this chapter, I will provide you with the agenda and processes for conducting your first board meetings.

7.2   We deliver

The first step when your Strategic Board meets is to review a draft of your Focused Intent as a group. I say a "draft" because you will gain their involvement to an even greater extent by taking the time to review each word and phrase of your Focused Intent. Allow them to clarify, understand, and question. Be open to any proposals they may have that refine and strengthen your Focused Intent.

> "If you tell people the destination, but not how to get there, you'll be amazed at the results."
>
> —GEORGE S. PATTON, GENERAL, U.S. ARMY

Let them assume ownership of the intent by developing a deeper understanding and personal relationship to your objectives.

Your initial Strategic Board process is iterative; members will collaborate with you in creating, reviewing, and revising. This is where the juice is. Listen to all proposals openly. Don't argue. Arguing will shut the process down. Pay attention, consider, and take advice and suggestions on board. Of course, you have the right to ultimately choose what will be done.

I have found one ground rule to be enormously helpful: the 90/10 rule. The meeting will flow when you invoke this rule for group discussion, by using the following process:

- Discuss points until they are 90% acceptable.
- The last 10% of agreement often takes most of the group's effort and isn't justified at this point, given that further steps in the process will demand refinement of executable actions.
- Reach tentative agreement on each issue, move on, and revisit the issues after more *offline* development by pathway pilots. These offline discussions will enable you and others to discuss specifics outside of the board meetings, thus sparing the entire group unnecessary deliberation.

You will find that the 90/10 rule allows people to proceed without getting bogged down in unproductive argument. Returning to issues at the next level of refinement often handles points on which the earlier conversation was snagged. Everyone experiences some degree of comfort when they understand that "we'll return to this point when we have to decide ..."

An objective of this first meeting is to determine what deliverables are required to fulfill each Pathway for Action. Charge your Board with the responsibility to identify and agree on the outcomes required for the success of each segment.

7.3   How come *outcomes*?

An *outcome* is a result. It is a quantifiable end state that you can specify in advance and that someone else can verify. It differs from an activity. An activity is action, often well intended, that is an interim step toward a result. The distinction between activities and outcomes is essential in setting and managing accountabilities. Steeled with this clarification, you can be brutally honest in identifying and recognizing the actual results to be achieved.

The following examples should highlight the distinction:

Activities	Outcomes
Having meeting	Established commitments
Developing budget	Approved budget
Taking training	Earned certification
Making presentation	Secured contract
Working on problem	Developed a solution
Assisting a customer	Satisfied a customer

In some cases, you can argue that an outcome is actually an interim step toward a final achievement. Or conversely, you might say an activity is a necessary prerequisite to producing outcomes. Apply your best Talmudic judgment. Keep your eye on the big picture.

I have rarely seen an organization in which people aren't busy. Everybody's busy, even in situations where the company's going out of business. Please note that busy isn't the same as productive.

You can usefully ask yourself or others four questions to clarify the purpose and importance of an activity:

- "Why am I doing this?"
- "Is this activity essential?"
- "How does what I'm doing produce what we are intending?"
- "Is there a better way to accomplish the same outcome?"

Your key to successful navigation of your Focused Intent is to steer toward results. Your board will keep you straight within the framework for producing results that you set up. Producing results and satisfaction that accompany such productivity will become the orientation of your High-Performance Operating System.

Spec Sheet 7.3 is designed for you and your Strategic Board to develop the deliverables that stem from your Pathways for Action. As well as "Outcomes" listed on the left margin, I have included other headings—*By When* (Due dates), *Specs for Success,* and *Dependency/Requests*—for you to enter others aspects of the deliverables later in this chapter. Instructions for each of these headings will be detailed as you address each one.

Start by writing the outcomes (1–3) for each *Pathway for Action* in *Spec Sheet 7.3*. Specifically write the outcomes that will occur in the next 60–90 days. This is important to get traction in each *pathway* in the short term so that you and others experience initial progress.

 SPEC SHEET 7.3—CLEAR OUTCOMES

Start by writing only the outcomes you intend for each pathway for action. Refer back to *Spec Sheet 6.2b* where you've already listed your initial ideas for pathways. We will complete the other columns as we proceed in the chapter. (Example responses are provided.)

By When	**Other *Specs for Success***	**Dependency/Requests**

Pathway A (*Sales*)

1. Outcome
(*new sales plan 4/15*)

2. Outcome
(*Train sales staff 5/1*)

3. Outcome
(*Report on results 6/30*)

	By When	**Other *Specs for Success***	**Dependency/Requests**

Pathway B (*Recruitment*)

1. Outcome

_____

_____

_____

2. Outcome

_____

_____

3. Outcome

_____

_____

Pathway C (*Funding/finance*)

1. Outcome

_____

_____

2. Outcome

_____

_____

3. Outcome

_____

_____

Pathway D (*Operations*)

1. Outcome

_____

_____

	By When	**Other *Specs for Success***	**Dependency/Requests**

2. Outcome

_____

_____

3. Outcome

_____

_____

Pathway E (*Product development*)

1. Outcome

_____

_____

2. Outcome

_____

_____

3. Outcome

_____

_____

Pathway F (*Research*)

1. Outcome

_____

_____

2. Outcome

_____

_____

3. Outcome

_____

_____

7.4   Get real

Before you proceed with the next steps in completing *Spec Sheet 7.3*, a little perspective will be useful.

More than 80% of the disruption in any organization results from a lack of rigor related to what I am calling Specifications for Success. These specifications are the conditions that if met will constitute successful completion of a commitment. By "disruption," I mean upsets, frustrations, and failed expectations. This hellish brew of aggravation is sourced in the default operating system. I am referring to good people working earnestly in a fog of assumptions. For the most part, they are able people who lack the clarity of speaking commitments and listening for commitments. In this wooly condition they appear unable to tolerate the discipline of clear and precise forethought.

> **"When you can measure what you're speaking about, and express it in numbers, you know something about it ... and you have, in your thoughts, advanced to the stage of science."**
>
> —Lord Kelvin, Physicist

In the High-Performance Operating System, the purpose of an (your) organization is to generate, coordinate, and fulfill commitments that are consistent with its (your) Focused Intent.

Yes, there are projects, and activities, and services. If you examine all that energy and motion under the magnification of a linguistic lens, what you see are people trading commitments but doing so imprecisely. These indistinct trades are occurring in every meeting, every sales call, and literally every form of interaction. People are intending to act, or they want action from others. However, seldom do these good folks clearly see these transactions and label them as commitments. This is business as usual in the indistinct *code* of the default operating system.

What elevates such usually vague expectations to explicit agreements is your clarity regarding the Specifications for Success. Here's a representative list to test commitments:

- By when?
- How will we measure?

- How many users will there be?
- What quality?
- How will the commitment be delivered?
- Who will be informed of the progress?
- What follow-up will there be?
- What will constitute closure?

These conditions once clarified build a basis of reality and reliability about what is requested or promised. Tune your High-Performance Operating System to listen for appropriate Specifications for Success that will underwrite the credibility of your commitments and the commitments of others.

Return to *Spec Sheet 7.3,* "Clear Outcomes." Once you and your board members have identified and agreed on what to include under the headings "By When" and "Other Specs for Success," write the relevant information in the space provided.

7.5   From dependencies to alliances

One more column in *Spec Sheet 7.3* remains to be filled. Before you complete "Dependencies/Requests," here is some additional background.

The success of almost all your results will depend on someone providing something toward the achievement of your Focused Intent. Most of the results you and others are signing up for are dependent on some contingent event where you rely on the action of another. Approval, conceptual buy-in, required funds, resources, applied skill, and expertise are all terminology for your dependencies to accomplish your stated outcomes.

In the alarm logic of the default operating system, dependency implies need. You will revert to forms of subtle manipulation when you are impelled by your needs. When others sense the concealed force of manipulation, they resist, often in the most polite and reasonable terms.

Other people care about forwarding their interests. In the action that flows from your High-Performance Operating System, you can shift need-based dependencies to supportive alliances. Convert your needs to commitments. Ask yourself "What commitment of mine is behind what I need?" For example, if you "need" administrative support, it is much more appealing for you to share with the person from whom you are asking assistance, the nature of the project on which you are working, and its importance to the business rather than how "swamped" you are.

Your commitments are much more interesting and accessible to others than are your needs. People whom you depend on will gladly become involved in your plans when you introduce possibilities to which they can connect. When other people can see the possibilities, they naturally move in the direction of expressing commitment. At this point, your "needs" and their commitments can converge. Once your interests come together, you can make *requests* appropriate to accomplishing your aims.

For example, address your dependencies on "marketing" or "finance" to a specific person who has the ability to act on your requests. Listen carefully to the way people speak about dependencies. "I need the approval of management." "I have to get the IT department to order me a new computer." More accurately stated, these fuzzy needs are weakly conceived requests that require other people to act on them.

I'll illustrate the process on enlisting support in more detail in Chapter 9.0. First, though, I want to look more closely at the nature of requests that issue from your High-Performance Operating System, as opposed to the needs that are a product of your default settings.

To recap, a request that is consistent with your High-Performance Operating System is an action in which you intend to obtain the clear commitment of another person. As the person making the request, you can use these common forms:

- "I ask"
- "Will you?"
- "I request"

By comparison, in the default operating system, "needs" are imparted as:

- "I need"
- "You need to"
- "I ought to"
- "You should"

The other person has three basic categories of response to a request:

- "Yes"—Acceptance: a *promise* to perform as agreed.
- "No"—Decline: a commitment "not to do what you've asked at this time."
- "Not that, but this"—Counteroffer: a conditional decline with an alternative offer for something that is acceptable. For example:
  - "This would be acceptable if ..."
  - "No. But if you were to ..."
  - "I will give you a definite answer tomorrow." This response includes deferring a response until another time.

If "yes" is to be credible, allow "no" as a valid option. If people can't say "no," then "yes" means nothing. In many situations, people don't think that they can say "no." Their unexpressed decline will show up at an inopportune time as failed or inadequate performance. "Yes" freed from any unstated resistance is a clear choice to perform as stated. It is not cloaked in "but, I didn't feel I could decline." Listen carefully for a "yes" that is not shaded with an undertone of reluctance: "Sure, (but) ..."

Your power is directly correlated to your ability to make big requests.

Your power is directly correlated to your ability to make big requests. The bigger the requests you make, the more dramatic the results you will initiate through stimulating your Network of Assistance. Your ability to make powerful requests is based on your confidence that what you are doing is important and worthy of the support of others. To operate at this level, you are required to get past your own self-limiting considerations, to stop delivering such lines as:

- "I don't have the authority to ask that."
- "No one has ever received ..."
- "What if they say 'No'?"

Communicate your Focused Intent in attractive and compelling terms. Go beyond the reasons in your own thoughts about why it can't happen. Your efficacy is directly linked to the strength of your conviction. The power of your intent will interest people. Move them to act toward your achievement by making empowering requests that they will accept.

If people decline your request, they haven't said that they reject you. All they said was "No" or (technically speaking) "I decline to accept what you ask, now." You can always approach them again with more relevant and compelling opportunities. When you have a sense they are enlisted in your proposition, you can make another request. Often you will get a different response.

Most of us want other people to be committed. Start a "virtuous cycle" by expressing your commitment. Your commitment evokes the other person's commitment. Phrase your request this way to elicit commitments:

- "I promise unprecedented results in this new project. I'd love for you to join me on the team this month. Will you?"

Detailed Specifications for Success (including "By When") will substantiate your commitments and requests, as I have discussed previously. We sometimes communicate weakly, thinking we've made a request. For example: "We ought to have lunch sometime." But we have not really said anything beyond expressing a vague obligation.

A more effective communication is: "I would love to get your input on an exciting new project. Let's have lunch on Tuesday. I'll make a reservation at Joe's Café for 12:30 p.m."

Once someone has accepted your request, make sure you acknowledge the commitment that has been created. Review what you have agreed to, and what follow-up you require, so all concerned are "on the same page." Written confirmation will eliminate lots of future grief.

> "To compromise in this matter is to decide; to postpone and evade decision is to decide; to hide the matter is to decide. There are a thousand ways of saying no; one way to say yes; and no way to say anything else."
>
> —GREGORY VLASTOS, SCHOLAR AND PHILOSOPHER

Once you've acknowledged the commitment, acknowledge the person who made it. "Thank you" extends the benefits of your High-Performance Operating System to that person. That person is likely to carry the acknowledgement in their interactions with you.

The last heading on *Spec Sheet 7.3* is "Dependency/ Requests." Indicate whom you and others are dependent on for each outcome. Once you've identified the person, clarify the specific request you want to make of that person. Return to *Spec Sheet 7.3* and complete the last column.

You now have framed your Focused Intent in clearly structured commitments tested within the matrix of your Strategic Board. You are now ready to roll!

STORE IN MEMORY

- Your Focused Intent matters enough to open your thinking and planning to how others might contribute. Once you realize you can't or, more important, shouldn't do it alone, you step up to a new, more inclusive platform of performance.

- Now you have an opportunity to include outside support and collaboration that will boost your achievements beyond past boundaries. Welcome to your Strategic Board.

- Your colleagues, friends, and others you admire want to be able to contribute to the achievement of your Focused Intent. In order to secure their contribution, you must act. Invite their participation, and structure a role for them in your success.

- The distinction between activities and outcomes is essential in setting and managing accountabilities. Steeled with this clarification, you can be brutally honest in identifying and recognizing the actual results to be achieved.

- In the High-Performance Operating System, the purpose of an (your) organization is to generate, coordinate, and fulfill commitments that are consistent with its (your) Focused Intent.

- Tune your High-Performance Operating System to listen for appropriate Specifications for Success that will underwrite the credibility of your commitments and the commitments of others.

- Your commitments are much more interesting and accessible to others than your needs. People whom you depend on will gladly become involved in your plans when you introduce possibilities to which they can connect.

- Your power is directly correlated to your ability to make big requests. The bigger the requests you make, the more dramatic the results you will initiate through stimulating your Network of Assistance.

- Most of us want the other person to be committed. Start a "virtuous cycle" by expressing your commitment. Your commitment evokes the other person's commitment.

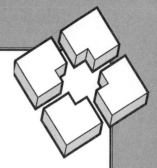

CHAPTER 8.0

The Right Tool ...
Move from problems to actions

"Expect problems and eat them for breakfast."

—ALFRED MONTAPERT, AUTHOR

 Preview

8.1 **Beyond where you stop** The purpose of your Strategic Board, and other components of your Network of Assistance, which we will develop as we proceed through *Choose What Works*, is to support you to go beyond the situations that stop you.

8.2 **What you ask for** In the edgy cycles of the default operating system, we have little patience for uncertainty, for tolerating the tension of not knowing. Instead, we mainly seek information to reinforce the answers on which we have previously settled.

8.3 **What's actually happening** Every professional discipline—law, medicine, engineering—values clear, precise observation and the establishment of facts as a necessary basis of rigorous practice. By contrast, we seldom apply vigorous inquiry to our business or personal life.

8.4 **Fields of possibility** You develop a field of possibility by making proposals. A proposal is an idea for consideration that can translate into action. It is what could be. They are intended to stimulate and inspire both you and others.

8.5 **Surf from "can" to "will"** People report some meetings as inherently satisfying, productive, and useful as they are able to connect to stated objectives, as well as to each other. Such meetings conclude with coordinated commitments, actions targeted to achieve a shared goal.

8.1   Beyond where you stop

Something stops you. I am not saying you aren't ambitious, hard working, and persistent. You have accomplished and will accomplish much. Yet, even highly successful people have temporary ceilings to their achievements. For some, the tether is a stifling judgment from others as to their capability. Others experience an unsettling defeat or the visceral discomfort of facing yet another unknown. The boundaries of what stops or blocks you may be varied or fixed, real or imagined. Where do you stop? What stops you?

The purpose of your Strategic Board—and other components of your Network of Assistance, which we will develop as we proceed through *Choose What Works*—is to support you to go beyond the situations that stop you. Let's examine the nature of those impediments and how you can be supported to go beyond reverting to historic patterns.

When you are confronted with problems that are barriers or stops to your Focused Intent, you have three primary choices:

1. **Indulge in unproductive assessment, emotion, or resignation**. The equivalent of kicking your car's fender and cursing shamelessly when the tire goes flat, this approach releases emotion. You can blame something or someone else for your misfortune. However, your car stays where it stopped. This option is the typical output of your default operating system.

2. **Cancel or change your commitment**. Always a "reasonable" option. In this approach, you can revise your agreements by listing all kinds of reasons, collecting supportive circumstantial evidence, or simply by saying you've changed your mind. You might say:
   - "I've had second thoughts."
   - "The situation has changed."
   - "I tried that, and it didn't work."

All these redirections will probably be legal tender in your or others' sense of business as usual. Remember, though, that even if you fool your audience, you can no longer mask the awful truth from yourself: these perfectly justifiable explanations are products of your default operating system.

3. **Commit to a powerful resolution.** This option sounds obvious and logical, unless you are in the midst of a situation that feels overpowering. Then, you are overwhelmed with the reactions, emotions, and default logic of what stops you. Committing to a powerful resolution when you don't see a traditional pathway forward takes courage, character, and a reliable framework for working toward new possibilities. The choice to act in the face of uncertainty is part of the *source code* of your High-Performance Operating System. This bold step is where you "go for it" in your resolve to accomplish your original commitment.

> Committing to a powerful resolution when you don't see a traditional pathway forward takes courage, character, and a reliable framework for working toward new possibilities.

Once you've crafted your Focused Intent, organized your Strategic Board, and agreed on your deliverables and dependencies, how effectively you resolve problems will determine your movement forward. As we discussed in Chapter 5.1, most problems you will encounter stem from your ambition. The greater your ambition, the more potential you've created for problems. Engagement with these problems is your playing field for progress. It is the margins that you've drawn to focus and accelerate your success. Acting decisively to resolve problems demonstrates your commitment to keep moving toward your objective.

 High-Performance Operating System—Cornerstone 3

Systematically identify and resolve barriers that are inconsistent with your intended results.

Systematic identification and accelerated resolution of problems are operations of high performance as you move toward your stated objectives. The heroic pursuit of your Focused Intent will ensure you a liberal stream of problems. Your skill in working with your board and employing useful tools to resolve these issues will make all the difference in building momentum.

> "The formulation of a problem is often more essential than the solution. ... To raise new questions, new possibilities, to regard old questions from a new angle, requires creative imagination and marks real advances."
>
> —ALBERT EINSTEIN, PHYSICIST AND NOBEL PRIZEWINNER

Convene your Strategic Board for a second meeting. The purpose of this meeting is transform problems into resolutions. Start by referring to the issues you converted to questions in *Spec Sheet 5.2c*, "Powerful Questions." These questions should still be relevant, though some may have evolved into the deliverables you shaped in *Spec Sheet 7.3*, "Clear Outcomes." Look over both Spec Sheets with your board, and prioritize the top two to three questions/problems, in the workspace provided below, that you want to bring into sharp focus.

My top questions/problems to resolve with my Strategic Board are:

1. _____

2. _____

3. _____

8.2   What you ask for

Now, turn your attention to *Spec Sheet 8.2*, which employs a useful method to move from problems to resolutions. The *Problem Resolution Methodology*, as I've called this approach, has four steps:

1. Express the problem as a *powerful question.*
2. State the current situation.
3. Generate proposals.
4. Agree on commitments to act.

Before you work through the four activities on this spec sheet, I will outline sufficient background for each step of the Problem Resolution

Methodology, so you understand how to gain the most from this effective tool.

Look over *Spec Sheet 8.2* (following page), "Problem Resolution Methodology." The four steps move us from complaint to coordinated resolution. The process is designed to succinctly and efficiently cover the essential processes for maximizing innovation and accelerated commitment. Each stage requires a specific format of discussion by your board to most effectively mine the desired outputs:

1. The team authors a "powerful question" in order to set a new context as the central focus their inquiry. Powerful questions develop the greatest opportunity for resolving the issue at hand.

2. The "current situation" is the first element I discussed previously when detailing the design of the High-Performance Operating System. In this stage, we rigorously reveal facts, relevant data, and people's directly reported experience as the basis of analysis.

3. Generating "proposals" is the engine for driving innovative and effective solutions. When the team members have expressed themselves without critical comment, they produce a field of possibility from which they can prioritize and select solutions.

4. The Problem Resolution Methodology is resolved by the team by "commitments to act." In this critical step "What we could do" moves to "what will we do." The powerful question is resolved in committed and coordinated actions by members of your board.

When I do this exercise with a group, I find that it works especially well on a flip chart or large whiteboard. If you have easy access to these materials, you may wish to complete the activity this way.

We will cover each step in detail as you proceed, allowing you to work methodically through the most pressing issues limiting the fulfillment of your Focused Intent. (Example responses are provided.)

(1) Powerful Question:

(How can I ensure adequate funding to sustain my start-up company?)

_____

_____ ?_____

(2) Current Situation	(3) Proposals	(4) Commitments to Act*
($15k in the bank now)	*(Save additional $45k)*	*(Put aside $3k per month)*
(Projected cash burn $30k per month for six months)	*(Attract investment for shares)*	*(Dev. investor presentation)*
(2 clients said they would be willing to work with us)	*(Ask for prepayment)*	*(Discount services for cash)*

* See Chapter 8.5 for expanded space to fully record *Commitments to Act.*

What is a *powerful question*?

Questions reframe the issues you identify and your approaches to solving them.

We have been trained since childhood to search for answers. We have a problem, and we want a solution. We have an impasse, and we want the ticket to smooth sailing. The quicker we get an answer, the better.

Questions reframe the issues you identify and your approaches to solving them.

In the default operating system, answers are the commodity we value. For instance, a client of mine attended one of the finest prep schools. He reported that in the competitive pressure to "look good," he never asked a question in class to which he didn't already have the answer.

In the edgy cycles of the default operating system, we have little patience for uncertainty, for tolerating the tension of not knowing. Instead, we mainly seek information to reinforce the answers on which we have previously settled. We experience comfort in knowing, even when there is little inner challenge to the veracity of what we have glibly accepted.

Questions that you formulate in your default operating system will not propel your understanding forward, as they are mostly limited to extending incrementally what you already know. Sometimes these questions are actually manipulative. I call them "statements with a hook on the end." For example:

What you say	What you really mean
"Don't you agree?"	I want your agreement.
"Why were you late?"	Get here on time.
"Do you have another solution?"	Tell me what I want to hear.

Your willingness not to have answers immediately activates the *portal*, or opening, to your High-Performance Operating System. Healthy curiosity replaces pat certainty. New questions arise in the face of new challenges. In this mode of creative thinking, you are eager to set aside what you know by reflex for what you might discover. This thoughtful process is termed *inquiry*.

Powerful questions set a new context for your inquiry and take you past your unexamined subtexts. Powerful questions develop the greatest opportunity for resolving the issue at hand. This order of question probes beyond what you and your board may take for granted or hold as "truth."

The following account shows how powerful questions can shape thinking and resolution for the greatest opportunity.

One of my clients was leading her team in a discussion of its Focused Intent. The company, which offered wireless telephone service, wanted to shorten the time that new customers had to wait for activation of service. I asked my client to formulate a question that was foremost in her concerns for the group to resolve. She offered, "How can we improve our activation process?"

"How long does it currently take for new customers to receive a dial tone?" I asked her.

"It averages 30 minutes," she replied.

"If you improved to 29 minutes' average time, would you feel we had accomplished something useful?" I asked.

"No," she replied.

"What do you really want?" I asked.

"I want an instant activation process when people sign up," she said.

"So can you think of a question that could open the team's thinking to achieve that result?" I asked.

"Um … What's required to provide instant activation to our new customers?"

She got it!

What difference do you see in the reformulated question?

In my view, this powerful question prompted the members of her team to look beyond incremental improvement and to question the status quo. Their responses motivated them to involve others. They moved past the scope of familiar routines and solutions. The team revolutionized the company's approach and set up an innovative company-wide project that led to virtually immediate phone access for new customers. The improvement would not have happened without the fresh opening that her question provided.

> "You can tell whether a person is clever by his answers. You can tell whether a person is wise by his questions."
> —NAGUIB MAHFOUZ, AUTHOR AND NOBEL PRIZEWINNER

As I previously instructed in Chapter 5.2, you begin the construction of a powerful question with "What" or "How."

Now to return to *Spec Sheet 8.2*, "Applying the *Problem Resolution Methodology*."

The first step in the Problem Resolution Methodology is to choose a problem or issue to work on as a group. Select one that you think would make the biggest difference if you were to resolve it now. State the problem as a powerful question in the space labeled (1).

8.3   What's actually happening

As you work through the Problem Resolution Methodology represented in *Spec Sheet 8.2* with your board, you will manage each step of the process differently. Each step will have specific ground rules for conducting and completing the discussion. Each step has defined ways of thinking and speaking that produce the intended effect.

Move to column (2), "Current Situation." Here's some required background to support your development of this step as an essential building block of the methodology.

Every professional discipline—law, medicine, engineering—values clear, precise observation and the establishment of facts as a necessary basis of rigorous practice. By contrast, we seldom apply vigorous inquiry to our business or personal lives. We have beliefs, opinions, and assumptions that are often products of our default operating system. Our default operating system selects and compiles evidence that matches our preexisting viewpoint. We report through the filters of strong emotion, sloppy language, or predetermined conclusions. This is not the invention of ignorant or dishonorable people. It is the product of a social hypnosis bred in unexamined code of the default operating system.

Transformation, a dramatic shift in perspective forged in your High-Performance Operating System, begins by discerning what's actually present. What's actually happening? What would you see if you looked at a videotape of the situation? What would be allowed as evidence in a courtroom? These and similar questions, such as the following, will help to determine the current situation.

- "What are the facts?"
- "What data is available?"
- "What is actually happening, or what happened?"
- "What is the evidence that supports this as a fact?"
- "What was said, literally?"
- "What did you or others observe?"
- "Is this an opinion or a fact?"

In order to establish the current situation, use uncommon levels of discipline in the way you and the board applies your listening skills to separate:

- Effect from cause
- What was said from what was heard
- Data from opinion
- Specific examples from generalized statements

Some examples will show you more clearly how you can shift ungrounded assessments (points of view without supporting data) to facts in order to build the current situation:

Assessment	Facts
"Our quota was too high."	"The quota was $75,000."
	"We achieved $62,000."
"They resisted our proposal."	"We offered X; they asked for Y."
"We don't have the funds."	"Our budget is X; the project costs Y."

"Management's view of us is negative."	"John Smith said 'X.'"
"She always does that."	"She did X on April 2; she did Y on May 7."

What are the differences when we state something as a fact rather than as an assessment? Facts have a number of distinct characteristics:

- In facts, we move from the general to the specific. "He always does" becomes specifically what was done and when.
- There are no "because" facts; individual data points and separate events are reported as disconnected observation. Broad assessments become discrete facts: "This happened" and "That happened." No cause and effect is assumed in the display of facts.
- Facts reflect no blame. Facts contain nothing for others to resist or contest. Facts are, by definition, verifiable—a matter of record.
- In facts, "What is" replaces "What isn't." For instance: "We don't have enough money" (a judgment) versus "We have X amount of money" and "We calculate that we require Y amount." What we have and what we require are two separate facts in a display of the current situation.
- Facts represent concrete realities and not vague characterization. As you sensitize your ability to separate evidence from interpretive description, you are able to identify what actually happened. The drama associated with situational "spin" is stripped away when facts replace self-justifying interpretation.

In this process of establishing the current situation, assessments and skewed judgments give way to details that aren't a matter of contention—claims you make confidently and positively that can be backed by data. Citing one clear example often has more power than making sweeping statements: "The employee survey indicates 78% of our people are not clear about our corporate direction" rather than "nobody knows where we are headed as a company."

"We don't see things as they are; we see things as we are."
—ANAÏS NIN, AUTHOR

Challenge your own or others' sense of victimization. Any time we act self-righteously or seek to make others wrong, we are demonstrating some level of victimization. Of course, we can more easily see others falling into this behavioral trap. The most telling phrases are generalizations that portray us or others as the injured party. Examples:

Complaint of victim	Responsible assertion
"We were robbed by the referee."	"The video replay of the game was open to a different interpretation by our team."
"Management doesn't care about us."	"Some employees feel decisions affecting them are made without their input."

Manage this step of the Problem Resolution Methodology by ruthlessly challenging assumptions. If you hear what sounds like an assumption, ask the speaker one or more of these four questions:

- "How do you know that?"
- "What was actually said?"
- "How could you state that as a fact?"
- "Do you have data to support that?"

You may notice that once you and others clarify what's actually happening, solutions rapidly emerge. Ideas for resolution often become strikingly obvious at this point. If someone offers a quick proposal at this time, manage the process and its inherent power by saying: "Hold that thought; we'll capture your proposal in a few minutes when we cover that step."

Managing this discussion and guiding the participation of others is a key component in establishing your leadership and the effectiveness of the board. People will often want to "chase after cars while barking down the street" at every topic that is identified. There is power and a surprising level of value in having people behave consistently with the rules of the process that you outline and enforce with them.

Your ability to create is the renewable resource within your High-Performance Operating System.

Discuss the current situation with your board now. Record the "Current Situation" (i.e., facts and data in column (2) of *Spec Sheet 8.2*). Noting 10 to 12 representative facts will be sufficient to establish a firm basis for proceeding to the next step.

8.4   Fields of possibility

Your ability to create is the renewable resource within your High-Performance Operating System. Our basis for creation is the dialogue we conduct with life. Knowing your intent and clearly seeing what's present in your environment yield opportunities to supply what's possible.

In the Problem Resolution Methodology, the powerful question you composed is your frame of reference. You are resolving your issue from your intent. The current situation of facts and data, arrayed against that background, is now present. You and your Strategic Board now have the opportunity to create a *field of possibility* that releases new ideas and actions.

"The best way to have a good idea is to have lots of ideas."

—LINUS PAULING, BIOCHEMIST AND NOBEL PRIZEWINNER

You develop a field of possibility by making proposals. A *proposal* is an idea for consideration that can translate into action. It is what could be. It points a way forward for your commitments but does not bind you to them. Intended to stimulate and inspire both yourself and others, a proposal is often expressed in these terms:

- "What if?"
- "How about?"
- "I see a possibility to ..."
- "I say we can"

Your only limit to generating possibilities is the editorial "hand-brake" of the default operating system. This brake, which is always concealed below the surface of the discussion, could be given voice by any board member. I call this "braking" action *voting*. Voting can be exercised silently or audibly. Usually people's vote is uttered as "Yeah, but." Voting can occur in the flow of an unmanaged discussion in a number of ways:

- "Yeah, but we tried that."
- "But that'll never work."
- "But how is what your saying different than my view (you put my idea down, so I'll follow suit)"
- "But I have a better idea."

This method of voting is potentially destructive because it occurs before any request for reaching a conclusion. Voting can undermine an idea or a new way forward because it is expressed prematurely and often goes unnoticed as a negative influence resulting in a mood of overly critical judgment.

Some ground rules will help you manage the discussion to build proposals with your Strategic Board:

1. The primary ground rule for this step is "No voting until we've registered all available ideas." Manage the strong pull to comment on or discuss each proposal at this stage. Questions for clarity and understanding are useful; however, resist voting on or modifying others' proposals. People will stop contributing if their ideas are vetoed at this point.
2. Anyone in the discussion can say anything he or she wants; however, each person is requested to finish speaking by making a proposal. For example: "I have been thinking about X, and it feels right. Therefore, I propose ..." or "I can't support that. So therefore, I propose Y."
3. Write down the proposal exactly as the person said it. Ask them whether you recorded the idea accurately.

4. Train yourself and encourage others to listen to the possibility of what is being proposed. The ability to receive the ideas of others creatively is an act of integrity within your High-Performance Operating System. You hear the ideas creatively when you can expand on the original proposal in your thinking. You do so with integrity, in that you are able to hear what they are saying as they intended it to be heard, and you honor their intent while you further develop the proposal in your understanding.

Really getting what someone else is saying has an additional accrued benefit. The people you've listened to will usually reciprocate by extending themselves to what you are saying and how you want to be heard. The conversation builds on itself.

The ability to receive the ideas of others creatively is an act of integrity within your *High-Performance Operating System.*

You are now prepared to produce a field of possibility by capturing the proposals of your *Board*.

Refer to the Current Situation, which you've already recorded or represented in column (2) of *Spec Sheet 8.2*. Use the "Proposals" column, which appears as (3) on the *Spec Sheet*, to record your and the board's proposals.

You can create proposals in a 1:1 relationship to each fact or data point.

For example:

<u>Current situation</u>	<u>Proposal</u>
"Our budget is X."	"Increase the budget by raising revenue forecast."
"The project costs Y."	"Reduce estimated project expenses for May."

You can also create proposals that account for two or more data points.

For example:

Current situation		**Proposal**
We offered X.	}	Hold a luncheon that builds greater understanding and trust.
They asked for Y.		

You will have a good sense when the "Proposals" column is complete. Further speculation will have a diminishing return; remember the 90/10 rule discussed in Chapter 7.2. You will discover the value of moving forward while the energy of the group is still vital. You will know when it's time to move on by the quantity and quality of ideas coming forward.

You and the board members can be relaxed about capturing all proposals and not voting on their merit. In the last step of the Problem Resolution Methodology, "Commitments to Act," you will ask specific individuals to act on a given proposal. At this final stage, you'll find out what's hot and what's not.

8.5   Surf from "can" to "will"

You can judge the usefulness of any meeting by a standard measure, "What got created?" You might respond to this question in several ways. For example:

- People delivered information. (information created)
- The team members understand their mandate. (understanding created)
- New members were introduced. (introductions created)
- The attendees were bored. (boredom created)
- The group had a lengthy and unresolved debate. (debate created)
- Each person made commitments to act. (commitments created)

People view most meetings as a waste of valuable time. They could be accomplishing something if they weren't stuck in a deadening meeting. They could be completing stalled work tasks instead of listening to unproductive talk. However, people report some meetings as inherently satisfying, productive, and useful. During these discussions, the participants connect their energies to the stated objectives and to each other. These meetings conclude with coordinated actions that aim to achieve a shared goal. Commitments are created in such situations.

This dynamic—people making connections and choosing to act—is a benchmark application of the High-Performance Operating System. Such meetings don't happen randomly. Rather, they are the product of a designed environment of focused energy and managed conversation. This is the environment in which your applied technology of high performance is brought into play.

Your second Strategic Board meeting, dedicated to working through the Problem Resolution Methodology, is at a critical stage. Members may be engaged, interested, even entertained. However, until somebody commits to act, the meeting and its central focus, your powerful question, will have no satisfactory resolution.

> "There is a request hidden in every complaint. There are results hidden in every request."
>
> —ARYNNE SIMON, MANAGEMENT CONSULTANT

The last step of the Problem Resolution Methodology is designed to harvest the output of the structured discussion you have conducted. In "Commitments to Act," you convert your proposals to clear and agreed actions. What could be done becomes what will be done. Talk moves to action. The future is specified in a clear set of conditions. Most important, you and those supporting your intent are mobilized to produce coordinated results through your and their choices.

Some information will support your efforts to manage this transition.

First, Commitments to Act are composed entirely of promises and requests. That's primarily what you register in column (4). Promises and requests are themselves actions in language. They are not descriptive of what has happened; rather, when you make a request or promise, you are causing something to happen by speaking. You are making commitments and listening for and eliciting commitments.

Second, promises and requests are the basic components of your High-Performance Operating System. The equivalent of the 1s and 0s at the core of a computer's coded soul, they function as building blocks of commitment assembled to establish and govern your commitments and performance.

Remember, individuals make promises and requests to other responsive individuals; departments and organizations don't speak to or for themselves.

In previous chapters, I've covered the various ways that requests and promises are applied and spoken in practical conversation. To review:

Requests	Promises
"Will you?"	"I will."
"I ask"	"Yes."
"Please do"	"Okay."
"I request"	"I promise to ..."

Third, if you and others are fulfilling every promise that is made, you are not generating promises from your High-Performance Operating System. You are in fact making predictions born in your default operating system. You and others supporting you will grow muscles for accomplishment when you accept challenging and creatively uncomfortable commitments. Responsibility is key here. This level of responsibility requires that you reconcile going for stretch objectives—challenging targets—without an easy way out if you fall short. This is an adult conversation; please don't interpret what I'm saying as an invitation to "try" and then fail. Trying, in this context, is placing the emphasis on the attempt rather than the result.

People seldom literally state promises and requests in terms of generating desired performance. Therefore, it is essential for you to listen meticulously to what people are really saying. What you say produces what you do; what others say is what they will do. For example:

"I'll try"	is not	"I will"
"I predict that ..."	is not	"I promise that ..."
"That's a good idea"	is not	"Yes"
"I understand"	is not	"I will act"
"Sure"	is not	"You can count on me to ..."
"I need"	is not	"I ask"
"It would be good if ..."	is not	"I request that ..."

> **"Nothing is easier than saying words. Nothing is harder than living them day after day."**
> —ARTHUR GORDON, AUTHOR

Commitments to act are commitments to perform. You are speaking to others within the currency of commitment. Committed speaking and listening are straightforward, no-nonsense ways of connecting with people and the results they intend.

Developing Commitments to Act requires the following actions:

1. Stand back and review the proposals that you and your board have recorded.
2. Prioritize the proposals that you think have the most merit. As the proposals with the most potential impact, they would likely be the carriers of more senior actions. You may discover that some of the other suggested actions on the list fit easily as components of the main proposals.
3. Ask the person who authored the prioritized proposal to restate it. Have the person elaborate the possibility they see. This person has the opportunity to sell the proposal to others in, say, a minute or less. When this person is finished speaking, the proposal will stand as a clear and compelling idea to be enacted.
4. Once everyone recognizes the value of the proposal, ask the person making the proposal whom specifically they are addressing. Is the speaker offering to carry out the proposed action on their own or asking someone else to act?
   - If the speaker is offering to perform the action, ask the speaker to specify the promise to the group. For example,

"I will prepare a complete presentation for the meeting on March 2."

- If the person is making a request for someone in the room to act, ask the speaker to make an actual request to that individual, now. For instance, "I request that you meet with the vice-president of Engineering by March 2 and secure the agreement for design services."
- The person to whom the request is addressed has three options to respond: accept, decline, or counteroffer. This is the moment of truth, where you find out whether something is worth doing. This is where the vote occurs. If the person accepts the request outright or accepts with modified conditions (counteroffer), this team member has committed to act. If the person declines and doesn't make a counteroffer, the requester can redirect the request to another person, or the speaker can offer to do it himself or herself.

  If accepted or modified as Commitments to Act, most proposals will be a composite of promises, requests, and counteroffers. This web of interdependencies requires close coordination and a spirit of cooperation among those harmonizing their actions.

5. Write your Commitments to Act in column (4) of *Spec Sheet 8.2.**

*To contribute to the continuity of follow-up and group clarity, *Addendum 8.5* (which follows), recording details for *Commitments to Act,* allows you to detail each Commitment to Act in four parts:

- **Person committing** (name of person promising action)
- **Result to produce** (the agreed outcome to be delivered)
- **By when?** (the date the result will be completed)
- **Specs for success** (e.g., How will result be achieved? What quality is required? What follow-up is called for? Who will be informed of progress and completion?)

Addendum 8.5   Recording details for Commitments to Act
(examples provided)

Person committing	Result to produce	By when?	Specs for success
(John)	*(Close XYZ contract)*	*(May 15)*	*(Value to exceed $40K)*

"Commitment is what transforms a promise into reality. It is the words that speak boldly of your intentions. And the actions which speak louder than the words. Commitment is the stuff character is made of; the power to change the face of things. It is the daily triumph of integrity over skepticism."
—AMERICAN EXPRESS, WALL STREET JOURNAL AD

Of course, not every proposal will be accepted or acted on. Something that seemed a good idea in the heat of a speculative discussion may have cooled in the shade of practical scrutiny or when someone realizes that someone actually has to act.

In the function of your High-Performance Operating System, you are working with a finite number of elements—promises, requests, and counteroffers—that lend themselves to an infinite number of applications. We will explore the extension of these elements to your initiatives as you proceed with achieving your Focused Intent.

STORE IN MEMORY

- Committing to a powerful resolution when you don't see a traditional pathway forward takes courage, character, and a reliable framework for working toward new possibilities.

- Systematic identification and accelerated resolution of problems are operations of high performance as you move toward your stated objectives.

- Questions reframe the issues you identify and your approaches to solving them.

- Your willingness not to have answers immediately activates the portal, or opening, to your High-Performance Operating System. In this mode of creative thinking, you are eager to set aside what you know by reflex for what you might discover. This thoughtful process is termed "inquiry."

- Transformation, a dramatic shift in perspective forged in your High-Performance Operating System, begins by discerning what's actually present.

- Challenge your own or others' sense of victimization. Any time we act self-righteously or seek to make others wrong, we are demonstrating some level of victimization.

- Our basis for creation is the dialogue we conduct with life. Knowing your intent and clearly seeing what's present in your environment yield opportunities to supply what's possible.

- You can judge the usefulness of any meeting by a standard measure, "What got created?"

- Promises and requests are the basic components of your High-Performance Operating System. The equivalent of the 1s and 0s at the core of a computer's coded soul, they function as building blocks of commitment assembled to establish and govern your commitments and performance.

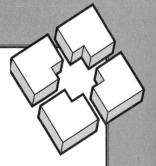

CHAPTER 9.0

Network Protocols
Fielding your web of support

"Miracles start to happen when you give as much energy to your dreams as you do to your fears."

—RICHARD WILKINS, AUTHOR

 Preview

9.1 **Intention + attention = results** What are you managing? Where do you fix your attention in pursuit of your intention? How do you combine preparation with desire?

9.2 **The moment of truth (the *Goldman Question*)** "Are you on track?" is the daily, weekly, and monthly moment of truth.

9.3 ***Heads-up Displays*** Graphic displays have authority. They give a quick read on where you and others stand and prompt early intervention to close disparities between goals and results.

9.4 **Your worldwide web** The resources you have to call on for assistance in realizing your Focused Intent can be surprisingly widespread. If you are able to extend this web of support, you can multiply your effectiveness.

9.5 ***HPOS* rules!** Your High-Performance Operating System works when you follow its rules. You have the opportunity to write the agreements that will govern your system.

9.1   Intention + attention = results

So far, your personal design work and your work with your Strategic Board have produced the following results:

- A statement of Focused Intent as the central navigation point of your vision
- A register of issues and concerns to be accounted for and resolved in subsequent planning and action
- Multiple Pathways for Action to guide high-level approaches to achieving your Focused Intent
- Assigned and agreed accountability and declared responsibility by your Strategic Board
- Specific outcomes and time frames by when key deliverables will be complete
- Identification of *interdependencies* that are required to support delivery of results
- Commitments to Act that originate as coordinated efforts to remove impediments to success.

Congratulations! You've written the prime components of your Personal Achievement Plan. For ease of reference, Appendix 1.0 consolidates of the above components in a "plan on a page" format. The one-page outline will aid you in assembling a cogent plan that you and others can implement.

In this chapter, we'll concentrate on common-sense project management and extending the assets that will support your achievement. In following chapters, we'll cover relationship strategies and communication skills more specifically.

You may feel that you require additional details in place before you can move forward. However, we are approaching the point where invoking the 90/10 rule will support your achievement. My coaching is to go forward when you've assembled 90% of your planning. As you launch into action, you will have opportunities to stand back from your plan, determine what's missing, and draw on additional real-world data.

When you resolve a problem through the application your High-Performance Operating System, you experience a renewed freedom to act. This freedom to act, guided in the Problem Resolution Methodology, is often experienced as a *breakthrough* in your ability to perform. In this sense, breakthroughs are more the opportunity to see and connect fully with a pitched ball than to actually hit a home run. In another domain of endeavor, a breakthrough for scientists in the lab may not be immediately finding a miracle cure so much as discovering an important new avenue for research. So, an initial skill you've been working toward is the ability to provide yourself with openings for action.

You are proceeding courageously and determinedly toward focused accomplishment. Once you begin incubating plans and accelerating actions at this early stage of advance toward your goals, it's time to ask yourself a useful question:

- What are you managing daily to secure your success?
  - Where do you turn your *attention* in pursuit of your *intention*?
  - How do you combine preparation with desire?
  - What does successful *execution* look like (beyond capital punishment)?

The following list might help you identify what you are managing:

- Your moment-to-moment frame of reference, mood, and motivation
- Your commitments
- The commitments of others
- The resolution of emerging issues
- Projects that target and track your progress
- Your communications

Yes, in succeeding, you will come to terms with managing all these elements and more. You will also find that the pat recipes and prescriptions prompted by your default operating system will be inadequate.

Instead, the framework provided by your High-Performance Operating System will present new practices, improved skills, and uncommon discipline to your accomplishments. Your thoughtfulness, authenticity, and integrity with others will serve you well in balancing the demands of the challenge. In addition, your sense of humor in dealing with obstacles and people will carry the day.

Your actions moving forward are now the tactical execution of your Personal Achievement Plan. Assigning and tracking this performance is *project management.*

In pragmatic terms, a *project* is a detailed plan with a beginning, a middle, and an end. It is bound in time and can be readily tracked. You start by knowing where you are, and the project then progresses through specific stages that build to the fulfillment of your stated objective. Seeing a project to completion is key. Too often, projects start and then meekly trail off into oblivion. When this happens, we rob ourselves of the benefit of close support and timely course corrections and of the satisfaction of closure.

> **"The test of a first-rate intelligence is the ability to hold ... opposed ideas in mind at the same time and still retain the ability to function."**
> —F. SCOTT FITZGERALD, NOVELIST

As Nobel prizewinning poet Czeslaw Milosz illuminates, developing and managing a project is to "cast an idea out ahead of yourself so that it gains autonomy and is fulfilled not only by the efforts of its originator but, indeed, independently of you as well."[2]

Project management is anchored from your Focused Intent and pulls today toward it. It is the secret sauce for managing continuity, complexity, and change. Project management permits you to think big thoughts and see the detailed management of tasks through to completion. It is an essential skill you can acquire in choosing what works. Project management receives precious little respect in the flash of dramatic business results or personal success stories.

---

[2]*Beginnings with My Streets: Essays and Recollections*, Czeslaw Milosz, Madeline G. Levine; Farrar Straus & Giroux, Feb. 1992

We want to approach project management with the appropriate touch. I am not talking about a burdensome binder with infinite details that blind you and others from responding creatively to what's happening on the playing field. Nor at the other extreme am I suggesting frivolous or fitful attempts to score a goal by just showing up and hoping something good will follow. I am suggesting a customized approach that works for you and that demonstrates efficiency.

Meet further with your board members. Your board at this point is a team that has co-ownership of the objectives that you've created together. Look at the deliverables and outcomes on which you and these colleagues have settled. Each one of these outcomes requires a detailed level of planning and alignment with other activities to meet the test of credibility.

Ask the following:

- What actions will you and they take to move from A to B, and from B to C, and so on?
- How will you and your team coordinate from where you are now to the agreed result?
- What processes and tools will you use?

Agree on a workable scale of project management and planning. The test is that project plans that you and your associates produce are presentable to and endorsable by others.

Select an appropriate instrument to schedule, track, and assess progress. You can use digital project planning software or a more traditional system such as a calendar and notebook. You and your colleagues can determine which system best fits your working style once you've dealt with the topic of project management head on. Whichever planning and tracking tool you choose, it should reflect the experience and accepted utility of your Network of Assistance.

Set a schedule of regular meetings to review progress and discuss issues. Your key to maintaining progress in a high-performance environment is to ensure that these discussions are fruitful and move forward crisply. Safeguard against getting bogged down in repetitive discourse. In some cases, the way forward may be governed by "do, learn, and reset plans." Getting into action, discovering what's working and what's not, and innovating using current experience and resources should offer a workable format. *Just-in-time planning* is a good name for the right balance between rigid formality and unstructured chaos. Even though you can't know every detail in advance, you can anticipate and plan for some eventualities. Keep your approach and process fluid, alive, and reliable.

The next part of this chapter covers a couple of meeting agendas that you will find useful in different situations. First, the reporting template in *Display 9.1* can help you discover the status of board members' actions and results. You can also use it to solicit agenda items from participants at the start of the meeting.

Display 9.1   *Strategic Board*—Progress Report

At the beginning of each meeting ask each board member to report on each of the following questions. No more than five minutes per person.

1. What is the Pathway for Action you are managing?

2. What was deliverable or intended in your pathway to date?

3. What did you accomplish? What's working?

4. Are your pathway commitments on track with agreed timelines?

    a. If yes, what supports that view?

    b. If no, what problems or impediments are you experiencing?

5. What could today's meeting most usefully accomplish to move your project(s) forward?

9.2 The moment of truth (the *Goldman Question*)

(I originally called the moment of truth the "Golden Question"—my clients corrupted its usage into the current form.)

The *Goldman Question* regarding project management is "Are you on track?" For many people trapped in the subjectivity of default logic, this query will elicit either glib assurance that all is well or a blank search for orientation stemming from no "track" to run on. The Goldman Question presupposes that you have a track to run on. Many people do not. "Am I on track?" is the daily, weekly, or monthly moment of truth.

> "Success is not the result of spontaneous combustion. You must first set yourself on fire."
>
> —FRED SHERO,
> ICE HOCKEY COACH

Being "off track" is often a temporary factor in carrying out projects. The internal guidance systems of aircraft navigate by sensing off-course movements and making subtle adjustments to speed, altitude, and direction. Course correction is the guiding principle of the Goldman Question, once you have positioned it as part of your High-Performance Operating System. This simple question is a potent tool.

Within a project management framework, the Goldman Question, "Are you on track?" will direct these additional questions:

- "How do you know?" ("What is your objective measure?")
- If "Yes," then "What's next?" ("How will you keep up the momentum?")
- If "No," then "How will you get back on track?" ("What's the revised plan?")

Display 9.2 (following page) shows the sequence of these questions. The query is also useful in self-management within a larger system of committed relationships, such as yours with your board members. The questions can act as a guide for your professional direction and daily priority planning.

Display 9.2   *Staying on track* - Project Management

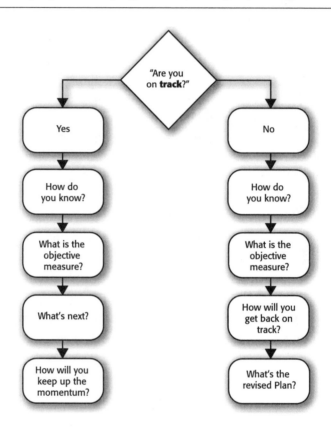

9.3   Heads-up displays

Graphic displays have authority. They serve as an immediate register of where you and others stand regarding your declared commitments. Simple, vivid displays communicate aspects of your current situation in unembellished terms. "A picture is worth ..." saves us from a thousand tedious stories. No justifications or pleadings to "let me explain."

I employ such graphics to demonstrate work in progress and call them *heads-up displays*. These useful exhibits give a quick read on your and others' progress to date and prompt early intervention to close disparities between goals and results. *Displays 9.3a* and *9.3b* depict two examples of effective heads-up displays.

Displays 9.3   *Heads-up displays*—Tracking projects at a glance

(a) "Key Milestones"

Task Name	Duration	Nov 01, 2003	Nov 25, 2003	Dec 09, 2003
DESIGN	18 days			
Verify Business Requirements	6 days			
Scoping Document	8 days			
Project plan	4 days			
Design Complete				
PROTOTYPE	18 days			
Detailed Design	4 days			
Implement Dimensions	4 days			
Implement Design	5 days			
Design Initial Reports	5 days			
Application Specification	5 days			
Prototype Complete				

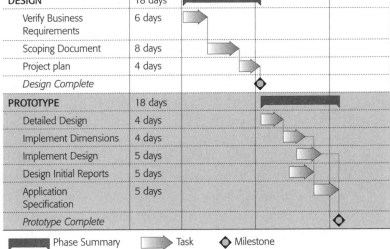

▆ Phase Summary   ▷ Task   ◇ Milestone

(b) "Releases"

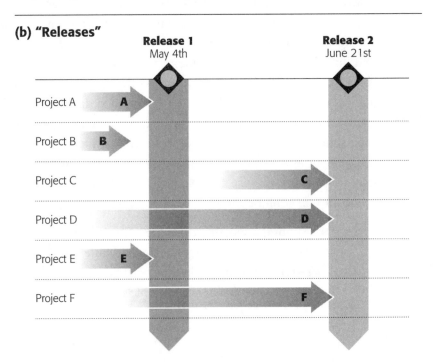

Heads-up displays that show (a) "Key Milestones" are valuable in tracking your progress toward your Focused Intent. Such a display allows you to plot interim deliverables. You can then readily determine how best you will manage convergent or conflicting events.

If others are working with you in parallel actions, then choose the "Releases" display, below. These displays depict the coordinating events that pull various streams of activity together. They can prompt members of your board to deliver outcomes to meet agreed and referenced events, such as next board meetings or customer visits. Events are more useful than dates in ensuring deliverables. Midterm exams always seemed to get my attention while just planning to study regularly never did.

Look over the deliverables for each of your Pathways for Action. Determine with your board members the "key milestones" and "releases" that will bring coordination and precise tracking to your activities. Build a simple yet effective display to represent these deliverables aligned in scope, timing, and committed outcomes.

Any type of medium will work for viewing your heads-up display. You can create the display on a computer using a range of project management or graphic applications. However, I have always found that simple is best—for example, a wall-mounted whiteboard with color markers. When you and your board review progress and reset plans, draw everyone's attention to the updated data on the heads-up display. Marking and acknowledging successful milestones completed is particularly energizing along your critical path to success.

When you review project work as part of project management, you may wish to use the use the meeting format shown in *Display 9.3c* (opposite), in conjunction with heads-up displays.

1. **Appoint a meeting manager** (This could be you).
   The meeting manager is responsible for delivering the required result within the specified time. This need not be the most senior or accountable person.

2. Agree on or create an agenda.

State the purpose of the meeting and its intended outcomes.

3. Find out what's working.

Report on achievements. Refer to the *Heads-up Displays* as relevant.

4. Discover what's not working.

Register issues and concerns. Prioritize issues, and pick the ones to resolve first.

5. Discuss what's possible.

Use the Problem Resolution Methodology to support creativity, buy-in, and structured solutions (see below).

Display 9.3c   *Project Review Meetings—Format*

Problem Resolution Methodology

Powerful Question:

Current Situation:	Proposals:	Commitments to Act:
_____	_____	_____
_____	_____	_____
_____	_____	_____
_____	_____	_____
_____	_____	_____
_____	_____	_____
_____	_____	_____
_____	_____	_____
_____	_____	_____
_____	_____	_____
_____	_____	_____
_____	_____	_____

6. **Record your Commitments to Act in a log.**
   Clarify Commitments to Act, their ownership, and follow-up steps:
   - Who owns the action?
   - What action is being taken?
   - By when will the result be delivered?
   - Other specs for success? (Remember these are the other conditions that constitute fulfillment of the intent and closure: What quality? Who will be informed? What are acceptance criteria? What pitfalls can be avoided? etc.)
7. **Thank board/team members.**
   Acknowledge people for their contribution to the meeting and the project.

Managing projects toward your Focused Intent is the daily bread of your High-Performance Operating System. Enjoy the meal.

9.4   Your worldwide web

The resources you have to call on for assistance in realizing your Focused Intent can be surprisingly widespread. If you are able to extend this web of support, you can multiply your effectiveness. Building this Network of Assistance will require you to express yourself through the medium of relationship.

Your commitment to conceive a bold intent and to take concerted actions that take you beyond your historic limits inspires other people in your life. Most are willing to associate with your success and offer assistance. For example, when my associate Laurie announced her plan to earn a degree in technical writing, her friends, family, and colleagues pitched in to make her Focused Intent become reality. A year and a half later, she had earned the degree, thanks in part to her colleagues assisting with computers, her friends taking over some of her daily chores, and her husband running carpools and cooking meals.

Once you've formulated your plans, let others know what you are up to. Your challenge is to move past the discomfort of communicating your aspirations. Select people who you think will appreciate your ambitions. Open lines of communication. Find out what they're doing, and then share your plans enthusiastically; it will invite their involvement in your success. My premise here is that people, given the opportunity, want to contribute to the commitments of others.

Even if communicating your aspirations is uncomfortable at first, I recommend that you persist. Once you've opened yourself to the contributions of others, you are likely to discover unexpected elements of support from this *Network of Assistance*—valuable information, helpful personal introductions, additional resources, and the benefit of others' experiences.

To help you identify who might comprise your Network of Assistance, survey the following potential categories:

- Board members
- Family
- Friends
- Business associates
- Organizations
- A designated coach

As you look over these categories of your Network of Assistance, select the specific individuals who can extend your resources and strengthen your probability for success, and enter this information on *Spec Sheet 9.4* (following page).

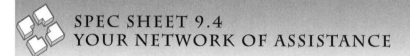

SPEC SHEET 9.4
YOUR NETWORK OF ASSISTANCE

Identify those people who could be part of your Network of Assistance, and specify the specific assistance you would value from each person. (Example responses are provided.)

Name of person	Specific assistance you would value
(John Samuals)	*(Gain skill in internet marketing)*
(Lisa Espisito)	*(Lessons on learning project management software)*
(Josh Patel)	*(Shared experience of alternate distribution channels)*

One tested idea can open up the discussion with others: share with them a draft of your plan or a written version of your current thinking. I emphasize the term "draft" as you are revealing a work in progress. You're inviting the viewpoints and ideas of other people to your planning process, so they will have a vested interest in your success. Remember Cornerstone 1 of the High-Performance Operating System: When people create something, they protect, nurture, sustain, and seek to fulfill it.

Once the person with whom you are discussing your plan is asking questions, making comments, and adding their contribution, you are in a position to request their participation as a contributor, advisor, coach, or board member. If the person declines your request, ask, "Whom do you think I should share my plans with?" See whether the person you are talking with will agree to arrange an introduction to another logical prospect in your unfolding network.

The benefits of this network of relationships will accrue to others, as well as to you. I've notices that among the most satisfying aspects of my consulting practice are accounts of clients who report that the ideas we covered in the conference room resonated beyond their original scope. Many of my clients claim that sharing approaches and solutions that initially applied to their work with family members and close friends had dramatic and unanticipated value. The ensuing discussions helped them work through previously unresolved issues and resulted in breakthroughs in other aspects of their lives.

As a striking example, one client participated in our professional discussions of approaches to support employees better and be receptive to their contributions. As this manager discovered how to accept the ideas and work products of stymied employees, he reported applying these same principles to his spousal and family relationships. His somewhat troubled marriage turned around, and his children developed a closer relationship with him. This client and others were able to see where they could extend what worked in one area of their life to other relationships. They placed openness and new opportunities for expressing themselves above the defense of rigid habits.

Similarly, you have the ability to use the tools of *Choose What Works* across the spectrum of your associations. You won't find any short circuits to instant mastery or any magic plug-ins for your High-Performance Operating System. But you do have a clear path to follow. Relationships developed through open and authentic self-expression are the royal road to expanding and maintaining your circle of influence and contribution.

You're worthy of people's time, energy, and involvement. They want to know that their contribution to you makes a difference. Let them know it does. The more you extend and feed your Network of

Assistance, the more you will flourish, along the way receiving both intended and unexpected benefits.

In the next chapter, I will coach you on how to compose and deliver communications that elicit greater cooperation and partnership.

9.5   *HPOS* rules!

Your High-Performance Operating System works when you follow its rules. You have the opportunity to write the agreements that will govern your system. The foundation for authoring and selecting these commitments is not random or erratic. It is embedded in people's sense of workability, trust, and honor.

Your High-Performance Operating System is constructed on a platform of integrity, of living true to your word and your values. Effective teamwork relies on the exchange of commitments. The clarity and significance of the commitments that you exchange with those supporting you affects your productivity and sense of purposefulness. You gain additional leverage toward the achievement of your Focused Intent when you and the people in your Network of Assistance treat their word as something to be honored.

You're worthy of people's time, energy, and involvement. They want to know that their contribution to you makes a difference. Let them know it does.

In my coaching sessions with executive teams, I at one time had the luxury of spending an afternoon encouraging groups to author a set of *Operating Practices*. These rules of engagement served as the foundational agreements for the team's ongoing relationships and performance. After many such sessions, I recognized that groups of people who work together, within the framework of High-Performance coaching, crafted strikingly similar ground rules. Team members from Scotland, Canada, Hong Kong, and Spain articulated the principles of "civilization" that demonstrated significantly parallel values.

After noticing the similarities, I refined my approach. Instead of asking people to compose their "constitution" on a blank piece of paper, I assembled the best common features and terminology of these

Operating Practices. *Display 9.5* gives the Operating Practices that I now use in my coaching work.

Display 9.5   High-Performance *Operating Practices*

1. I will take a clear stand for the possibilities and effectiveness of my/our Focused Intent and will express that stance consistently to others.
2. I will actively acknowledge my/our accomplishments toward realizing the Focused Intent.
3. As a priority, I will schedule time for dedicated Strategic Board meetings and project work.
4. I will reply to communications from board members in the following response times:

    Voice _____   e-mail _____
5. I will be on time and prepared for any scheduled meetings, phone calls, or other agreed-on commitments and will acknowledge to team members any unfulfilled promises that I have made.
6. I will act appropriately to communicate or correct inadequate performance from others or myself rather than overlook it.
7. I am willing to be coached in a direct and straightforward manner.
8. I am willing to offer a coaching relationship to my colleagues and team members.
9. When I observe complaints, I will turn them into powerful requests for action and address the requests to someone who can act on them.
10. Where my work calls for the contribution of others, I will enlist their participation or respectfully allow them to decline.
11. I will speak and act respectfully to all board/team members recognizing that everyone is an extension of my Network of Assistance.
12. I agree to responsibly resolve all issues and problems in my area of accountability within the framework of these agreements.

When I submit these Operating Practices to current groups, I say something like: "I am offering these sample Operating Practices for your consideration. I don't think you should necessarily adopt and follow these rules, but you may wish to do so. I ask that you first discuss the rules within your team so that you are clear what they say and understand what they imply. Once you appreciate the rules and their consequence, you are free to adapt them to suit your experience and intentions. You can accept all or some of them, modify them, reject them, or write your own rules. If they are to serve as your Operating Practices, they must reflect your values and your process of governance and self-regulation. OK, start your engines." I then ask them to meet to decide on their Operating Practices within a given period.

> "We must be the change we wish to see in the world."
> —MAHATMA GANDHI, INDIAN ACTIVIST

I offer these Operating Practices to you under the same conditions I communicate to the teams of executives whom I coach. Read them over thoughtfully. Discuss and agree on their implications with your board members. Choose to use or modify them as you wish. Beyond your board, you can offer and apply them to your other important relationships such as project teammates and people in your Network of Assistance.

Most groups accept the Operating Practices with few or no changes. The time frames for voice and e-mail responses are usually one business day or sooner. When they have finished discussing and adapting the Operating Practices, I caution the groups not to pass them along to others in their organization without working with them for 30 days first. Once we've reviewed them at that point, they are free to extend them to colleagues, family, or friends.

I encourage you and your board to keep your Operating Practices handy and refer to them regularly to deepen their relevance and meaning.

The parable that follows vividly signifies the rationale for not imposing or sharing your agreements with others until you have worked with them and incorporated them to your High-Performance Operating System.

A woman sought an audience with Mahatma Gandhi when he was an esteemed leader of India. She brought her 8-year-old son with her. When she was finally granted a few minutes to speak to the national hero, she pleaded, "Please tell my son not to eat sugar."

Gandhi looked at the boy, reflected on the appeal for a moment, and then turned to the woman and said, "Please return to see me in two weeks." The woman bowed politely and left with her son.

Two weeks later, the woman reappeared at Gandhi's study and reminded him: "Mahatma-ji, I was here a fortnight ago and requested that you instruct my son not to eat sweets. You told me to return today." Gandhi now looked at the lad and said firmly, "Don't eat sugar!"

The woman thanked him deeply and started to leave. She paused for a moment and said, "Sir, I mean no disrespect, but why did you have me return in two weeks?" With a characteristic twinkle in his eye, Gandhi replied, "Madam, two weeks ago I ate sugar."

STORE IN MEMORY

- You are proceeding courageously and determinedly toward focused accomplishment. Once you begin incubating plans and accelerating actions at this early stage of advance toward your goals, it's time to ask yourself a useful question: what are you managing daily to secure your success?

- Your actions moving forward are now the tactical execution of your Personal Achievement Plan. Assigning and tracking this performance is project management.

- Project management is anchored from your Focused Intent and pulls today toward it. It is the secret sauce for managing continuity, complexity, and change.

- For many people trapped in the subjectivity of default logic, "Are you on track?" will elicit either glib assurance that all is well or a blank search for orientation stemming from no "track" to run on.

- Simple, vivid displays communicate aspects of your current situation in unembellished terms. "A picture is worth ..." saves us from a thousand tedious stories. No justifications or pleadings to "let me explain."

- Your commitment to conceive a bold intent and to take concerted actions that take you beyond your historic limits inspires other people in your life. Most are willing to associate with your success and offer assistance.

- Relationships developed through open and authentic self-expression are the royal road to expanding and maintaining your circle of influence and contribution.

- The foundation for authoring and selecting your Operating Practices are not random or erratic. It is embedded in people's sense of workability, trust, and honor.

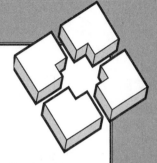

CHAPTER 10.0

There Shall Be Coaching
Are you coachable?

"I want to stay as close to the edge as I can without going over. Out on the edge you see all kinds of things you can't see from the center."

—KURT VONNEGUT, AUTHOR

 Preview

10.1 Let coaching in Valuable coaching relationships are not designed to fix something that's broken. Instead, they operate from the notion that you are already whole.

10.2 Coaching—isn't and is Coaching is predicated on improving performance to a level that someone has said they want to achieve. It is not therapy. A good coach is not a cop, a nanny, or a surrogate player. There is no universal form for doing coaching the right way.

10.3 Hire your *higher* In what areas of your work and life are you requesting coaching? With whom could you develop a coaching relationship? How do you find a coach?

10.3 The character to win The character to win is your resolve to manage the default logic and related devices that reduce and undercut the power of your commitments. When you understand the nature of these default processes, you are free to exercise the authority of your word.

The phenomenon of coaching has emerged as an increasingly accepted practice in business and other pursuits. The term "coaching" is applied to a broad array of activities and situations. Our concern here is to define effective coaching and how you can most benefit from its application toward the success you've defined in *Choose What Works.*

10.1 Let coaching in

How would you feel if you already fulfilled your objectives for success? Imagine how you would be if you had reached your intended destination. If you had nothing to prove, no struggle or challenge to overcome, how would you behave? What would your life look like if you could live and work from a state of satisfaction and creative reception to the current circumstances?

These propositions represent the perfect conditions of openness for coaching to flourish. When you are least distressed, you can gain the most from masterful coaching. Your High-Performance Operating System has the switch set to "receive." However, it is unlikely that we could reside in such a state for long given the pull of our default operating system.

Rather than being need based, this level of coaching is founded in possibility. The relationship is formulated and tuned to the achievement high performance.

This notion of an exquisite acceptance sounds contrary to conventional wisdom. "You can't coach someone who doesn't have a problem" is an old saw in consulting circles.

We usually seek coaching when we have a crisis or are thwarted in attaining something we want. In such situations, we are desperate for advice and strain to listen for the "answer" as a balm to our current dilemma. Seeking immediate answers is certainly our quest for coaching when we are lost in the caverns of our default operating system. I call this demand *need-based coaching,* and it has only incremental usefulness, in that it satisfies our seeking escape from a current dilemma, yet insignificant enduring skills are gained.

However, another prototype of coaching is a great deal more effective. In this case, the coaching is based on a strong relationship, one that is dedicated to improving and sustaining performance. All world-class performers—athletes, opera singers, and politicians—enjoy coaching relationships. These relationships are not basically designed to fix something that's broken. Instead, the coaching is offered and accepted from the notion that you are already whole. Rather than being need based, this level of coaching is founded in possibility. The relationship is formulated and tuned to the achievement of high performance.

> **"Discovery consists of seeing what everybody has seen and thinking what nobody has thought."**
> —ALBERT VON SZENT-GYORGYI, NOBEL PRIZEWINNER FOR MEDICINE

These coaching relationships rest on the assertion that you and I benefit from the perspective of others. In the open dialogue that characterizes these relationships, we are able to see what we are normally blind to—our "back swing," where we are stuck or where we fall short of operating in the "zone" of peak execution. The coach sees what's missing in our performance, not what's wrong about us. "What's missing?" This question stimulates a creative inquiry within the framework of the coaching for something that can be first observed or imagined and then developed.

10.2 Coaching—isn't and is

Most people I meet are not reluctant to offer "coaching" to someone else in unfortunate straits. These well-intentioned folks are most willing to provide what they call "coaching." The following section looks at what is "off" about the default logic of their efforts and how they missed the mark.

What coaching isn't

Without a relationship in place that is based on respect, trust, and receptivity, coaching can't occur. If someone doesn't appreciate that you're "for" them, almost any feedback you offer will seem threatening. "He told me that my presentation was fine; now what did he mean by that?" However, if people believe that you really care about their welfare and are on their side, they will listen to and consider almost anything you say—including comments that reveal the awful truth. "He said my presentation missed the mark, that I could have closed with a strong request for the order. He was right."

Ironically, people are least receptive to all forms of coaching when they seem to most require a way forward. When they are "gone"—submerged in the depths of their default-dictated reactions—they can't hear even the best-positioned counsel. When I am frustrated, angry, or sad, I am hardest to approach and usually closed to suggestions for effective action. A strong bond in the relationship and agreements about how to stay open to support in these circumstances will usually prevail.

In most cases, these misdirected attempts at coaching are "advice giving." People offering this form of what they consider coaching are supplying answers and solutions to questions that aren't being asked. They are pouring advice into a human vessel that is either already filled with distractions or unreceptive to input.

What coaching is

Coaching is predicated on improving performance to a level that someone has said they want to achieve. It is not therapy. A good coach is not a cop, a nanny, or a surrogate player. There is no universal form for doing coaching the right way.

We often wear many hats in our relationships with others, and knowing what role and degree of support we're providing is useful. Specifically, coaching is distinct from leading, managing, mentoring, consulting, and training, which we can define as follows:

- Leadership: shaping and directing change for and with others
- Management: stabilizing and implementing action to regulate operations
- Mentoring: guiding, educating, and counseling a less experienced person

- Consulting: supplying requested advice, expertise, or specific results within a explicit contract
- Training: applying a process of skill development for replicable application
- *Coaching*: is in contrast, a relationship dedicated to agreed performance improvements

Coaching is permission-based. The question "May I offer some coaching?" is often an opening for the coach to contribute. Skillful coaching shifts the perspective and awareness of the performer and brings to light fresh choices.

What a coach does

Questions are generally the most effective way of initiating and managing a coaching conversation. Although not an ironclad rule, questioning offers a reliable protocol to follow in building rapport and a foundation of trust—for example:

- "What actually happened?"
- "What occurs for you?"
- "What have you found that worked?"
- "Where are you stuck?"
- "What solutions haven't worked?"
- "What's missing?"
- "What outcome are you seeking?"
- "If anything were possible, what would you choose?"
- "What options do you see?"
- "Have you considered?"
- "Who could support you?"
- "What requests do you have (and of whom)?"

Coaching requires looking at the "player" in the conduct of their "game." It is a way of seeing, relating, and communicating that alters awareness and raises performance on the "field of play." Once the relationship is established and validated in the experience of the person receiving the coaching, the coach has permission to supply a broad array of support including suggested actions, cautions, recommended approaches, and yes, information and advice. The difference now is there is an empowering context for performer to hear all this in meaningful ways.

A coach communicates in a way that produces opportunities for the performer to see new possibilities:

- The coach's actions are based on the commitments of the player rather than what the coach wants for the player.
- The coach and the player base their relationship in the dynamic of their High-Performance Operating Systems. The coach sees the game differently than the critics and the casual observers on the sidelines. With no stake in the game, the observers and critics usually trade in assessments and evaluations crafted in the default operating system.
- An expert coach crafts their communication to expand the ability of the player to take new and distinct actions.

The criteria to judge the effectiveness of a coach are measurable improvements in performance on the "field of play." If the players aren't ultimately succeeding, it is preposterous for the coach to claim that they got the job done. "Well, I gave good advice ..." Coaching is about results, not about the quality of the information exchanged or the reasons for the coaching not working. This acceptance of ultimate measures of effectiveness is the code a coach lives by.

In fulfilling your Focused Intent, you will substantially benefit from establishing a formal coaching relationship. I urge you to add to your Network of Assistance a person who is qualified, interested, and appropriate to act as your coach.

10.3 Hire your *higher*

- In what areas of your work and life are you requesting coaching?
- With whom could you develop a coaching relationship?
- How do you find a coach?

Responding to these three questions will lead you to the person(s) who can most contribute to you now. Start by asking members of your Network of Assistance whom they might know or can recommend. Ask people you admire whom they can suggest as coaches. Tune your personal search engine to the three questions, and you will soon have several options to investigate.

Spec Sheet 10.3 will help you examine how you could most effectively select an appropriate coach and prepare you for gaining maximum value from the relationship.

SPEC SHEET 10.3
YOUR COACHING SPECS

Respond to the following: (Example responses are provided.)

A. In what specific areas would you most request coaching?
Technical skills

(Internet marketing) _____

_____

_____

Business skills

(Raising investor financing) _____

_____

_____

Communication/relationship skills

(Getting to "yes" without manipulation and force) _____

_____

Management skills

(Retaining good people)

_____

_____

B. What do you see as the greatest risks and barriers in fulfilling your Focused Intent (experience, time, limited resources)?

(Attracting cash and customers)

_____

_____

C. What would you most value in the coach's approach (discipline, no easy "passes," humor) and level of support (intensive, occasional, upon request)?

(Tell me when I'm "full of it!")

_____

_____

D. What do you most resist in being coached? In what areas of your life (e.g., smoking, exercise, diet, temper) aren't you supportable?

(Listening to advice when I'm angry or frustrated; asking for directions!)

_____

_____

E. Who would be an ideal coach for you? Name *(Paul Jamison]* _____

Experience *(Built successful marketing firm)*

_____

_____

Skills

(Knowledge of the business marketing and how to run a start-up company; patient, wise)

_____

_____

After you've selected a prospective coach, meet with him or her and review these points:

1. State what you would most value from the relationship.

2. Outline your Focused Intent and then ask what experience the prospective coach has that they consider to be most relevant.

3. Discuss how much coaching time will be appropriate to support your efforts. The length and frequency of sessions may decrease as you move closer to your goals.

4. Determine how both of you will assess the effectiveness of the relationship. How will you know whether the coaching is having the desired impact?

5. Find out what the prospective coach thinks are the most significant barriers you have identified to achieving your Focused Intent. Given what is currently foreseeable, how might your coach reinforce your ability to succeed?

6. Do you feel comfortable with this person? Are you inspired by the prospect of working with them? Identify any areas of sensitivity (e.g., confidentiality) that may be relevant.

You can ensure a more effective coaching relationship by setting the right specifications for success. If you decide to work with the coach, you can use their responses to create effective agreements for your coaching relationship.

Early in my career as a consultant, I was managing the productivity of 27 associates. I had reached what I felt was the limit of my skills and my patience in producing further results with the team. I decided I would hire a consultant/coach to "get the team more productive."

The prospective coach waited patiently while I went through my list of things I wanted him to "fix" with the team. Finally, he asked for a check to start the work. I signed it and handed to him. He calmly walked over and closed the door to my office and said, "OK, we are going to begin the project by going to work with you."

As in the instance above, the direction or focal point of the coaching may be significantly different from what you envision at the outset. I learned that I was blind to some of my behaviors, especially my insistence on certain methods to produce results from the team. I was using the force of my authority, and my arrogance about how I got the job done when I worked in their positions, as an arsenal of my default operating system. I couldn't see the counterproductive impact of my growing frustration on the team's morale.

In the final analysis, I saw that I was hiring this coach not for his knowledge of my business but for the perspective he offered. He was more alert and awake to the issues to which I'd stopped paying attention. Thanks to his input, subtle shifts in my approach and presentation with the team produced dramatic gains in their productivity and satisfaction.

Make your primary objective to have your coach succeed brilliantly.

My experience showed me that if something isn't happening in my environment, I am likely to have a prime connection to its cause and resolution. Understanding the nature of coaching and being open to the coaching are essential factors in the success of this undertaking. Stay open to the process.

Display 10.3 outlines a simple format that you can follow for one-on-one meetings with your coach to manage and accelerate your results. This template is also useful in anticipating the types of interactions you might have with your coach; you can apply that thinking when you work through barriers between coaching sessions.

Another tool that will underwrite the success of your relationship with your coach is maintaining a *coaching journal*. Use the journal to track actionable outputs of the coaching sessions. The primary value is to maintain a brief yet complete record or "database" of commitments you have generated and achieved in your work with the coach. Make it a habit to review the status of these commitments on a regular basis. It will keep you paying attention to how your coaching interactions propel you toward your objectives. Develop a coaching journal by entering the following headings in a notebook.

Display 10.3   *Results Management*—Meetings with Your Coach

1. Share what's working.

2. Identify the current issues to address.

3. Address: "What's stopping me from moving ahead on projects that will deliver my Focused Intent?"

4. Work with the coach to resolve the issues:

   a. Discuss: "What's possible?"

   b. Determine: "What actions can I now take?"

5. Ask: "What can I do to raise the level and/or pace of achievement of these projects to make the greatest impact toward my Focused Intent?"

Here are the six main headings for your coaching journal: (Example responses are provided.)

- Contact date *(6/15/03)* _____

- Past commitments I achieved/didn't yet fulfill *((+)Hired assistant, negotiated new salary; (-) professional training plan incomplete)* _____

  _____

  _____

  _____

- Issues discussed *(Elements of personal training plan; How to manage assistant)* _____

  _____

  _____

  _____

- Issues resolved *(Professional training plan completed)*

  _____

  _____

  _____

  _____

- Commitments I made *(Start new assistant with adequate resources and clear direction)* _____

_____

_____

_____

- Date/time of next contact *(6/22/03)* _____

The meetings you hold with your coach hold the promise of releasing your performance to new and satisfying levels. Remember, something is created when you speak and in how you listen. Coaching is the creative tension between what you currently know and what is possible.

> "The moment one definitely commits oneself, then providence moves too. All sorts of things occur to help one that would never otherwise have occurred. A whole stream of events issues from the decision, raising in one's favor all manner of unforeseen incidents and meetings and material assistance, which no man could have dreamed would have come his way."
>
> —JOHANN WOLFGANG VON GOETHE, POET AND PHILOSOPHER

I do not personally believe that "everything" is possible. However, something is possible beyond what I maintain today. I endeavor in my relationships and in my daily thinking to be awake to where I'm "positioned" against other possibilities and get out of the way.

To make the most of the coaching, move your default operating system aside. Allow your high-performance self to emerge from underneath the furious quest to preserve your default identity. If you find yourself closing down or becoming solidly resistant, see whether this is a pattern of default behavior that you are willing to get beyond. You are most likely pushing against the boundary between the legacy of your habits and the person you can become. Consider your relationship with your coach as a portal to your High-Performance Operating System.

Coaching is an interactive process. It is your invitation for honest feedback from the world. Respect what is said. Be coachable. Take the information on board without arguing or manufacturing explanations. Your coach is speaking to the person you intend to become. Make your primary objective in this relationship to have your coach succeed brilliantly.

10.4 The character to win

When you have initiated coaching in your life, you are likely to discover that learning will emerge from the most unlikely sources: the experience of others or books and articles that jump out at you. It's as if you are tuned to a new station in life that is broadcasting directly to you. You're selecting and attracting information, experiences, and people that resonate with your Focused Intent. As you remain purposeful, you will see and integrate the opportunities they represent into your plans, actions, and results.

How to stay on track yet alert to collateral influences is an interesting question of priority and balance. Pat formulas and glib recipes for success give way to your own sense of equilibrium and proportion as you work toward your goals. Some of the operating instructions for the "advanced" levels of your High-Performance Operating System at first can seem paradoxical. Further reflection and discussion with your coach and your Network of Assistance will reveal the ways forward. To aid you, I have included some additional thoughts to bring to those somewhat complex points of discussions.

First, it is essential to remain extremely goal oriented while at the same time not being rigidly attached to every outcome.

Second, use pragmatic, step-by-step objectives for concentrated effort and tracking. The progressive achievement of these short-term goals is imperative, yet they never mechanically add up to the total of your Focused Intent. That intent is a larger and richer frame of reference than the sum of its individual tactical components.

Third, the bigger context for winning includes having goals but not being blindly gripped by results or immediate success or failure. When you do something well and are applauded for it, you run the risk of becoming complacent and not learning new skills. In contrast, your interim failures can cause you, either with your coach or alone, to confront what's not working and to pierce through old patterns. In this sense, facing and resolving breakdowns are the path to breakthroughs.

Finally, being a student open to the world around you is a path toward greater success and accelerated learning. Your affirmative attitude, your enthusiasm, and your openness to receive contributions from your environment are priceless assets. The pursuit of your Focused Intent is an occasion to meet new challenges and feel the excitement of a "beginner." Your willingness to learn anew is an invitation to experience the curiosity and wonder of how you create in your life. When you are fully engaged in the daily process of designing and moving toward achievement, work and play merge. The passion of being fully alive on a field of play of your choosing offers its own reward.

"Being good in business is the most fascinating kind of art."
—ANDY WARHOL, ARTIST

Most of us are highly skilled at various common daily tasks. Peeling an apple, tying our shoes, or typing on a keyboard were once daunting skills that became encoded in our nervous system through repeated practice. Now, we are able to perform these activities almost automatically. The same processes of moving through the unfamiliar and establishing new patterns of performance are called for in meeting your current challenge to succeed.

Working with your *source code* of commitment, you can expand your capacity to meet added demands and incorporate newfound skills. As your work progresses toward fulfillment of your Focused Intent, you are challenged to do the following:

- See innovative solutions to familiar problems
- Observe yourself in your *default* mode
- Override old subtexts with new frames of reference
- Be accountable and responsible
- Settle unfocused discussions with commitments to act
- Stay receptive to coaching.

The character to win is forged in bringing ourselves, in part through coaching, to these new practices with insight, determination, and persistence.

Our commitments and the commitments of others on whom we depend are tricky to manage and sustain. These commitments persist as a function of our personal relationships with their significance and existing relevance. Therefore, they don't reside in a *stored system*, like the hard disk on our computer. The moment commitments are generated, they begin to degrade and are subject to incomplete recall and distorted interpretation. I call this phenomenon the *half-life of commitments*.

After you make commitments or accept those of others, three factors can reduce these promises to act:

- **Time.** The longer the period between your creation of a commitment and its review and "re-creation," the greater the likelihood that the commitment will weaken. ("Re-creation" is the process of energizing a commitment with its original intent.)
- **Geography.** Distance reduces the power and immediacy of commitments. Out of sight, out of range.
- **Default logic.** Left to its internal logic, the default operating system will systematically undermine the clarity and conviction of your commitments. Although this insight isn't complimentary, it represents a reality to confront and override. Pay attention when you find yourself saying something like the following:
  - "Well, I accepted that because I felt I didn't have an option."
  - "Things have changed."
  - "This is a lot more work than I anticipated."
  - "I don't feel the same way I felt then."

The character to win is your resolve to manage the default logic and related devices that reduce and undercut the power of your commitments. When you understand the nature of these default processes, you are free to exercise the authority of your word. In doing so, you build the platform to maintain your commitments rather than simply accommodate your moods. In practicing and strengthening your relationship to your word, you gain an extraordinary edge, an uncommon sense of freedom, and a new sense of yourself.

"If you don't have a strategy that people own and can act from, you will be permanently reactive and part of someone else's strategy."
—ALVIN TOFFLER, FUTURIST

As you restore or develop your integrity, the quality of fidelity to your word, you will start to notice that the circumstances have much less influence on your actions and results. In turn, your integrity and commitment will have a restorative effect on the environment and the mood. People in your Network of Assistance and elsewhere start to dance to the tune you're playing. Those who are not ready for or interested in the challenge of the new way of doing business with you will gradually "deselect" themselves from the game. The deadening conspiracy that characterizes many social contracts—"Don't call me on my shortcomings, and I won't call you on yours"—will quickly dissipate.

Along the way, you will find out whom you can depend on and whom you can't. Be supportive yet clear about your specifications for success with others. You will discover that engaging in conversations and relationships that don't produce commitments no longer satisfies you. Concentrate on walking the talk, and others will follow your example. Your courage, with the aid of your coach, to reinforce the practical applications of your High-Performance Operating System underlies the character to win.

STORE IN MEMORY

- Effective coaching is based on a strong relationship, one that is dedicated to improving and sustaining performance.

- Rather than being need based, this level of coaching is founded in possibility. The relationship is formulated and tuned to the achievement of high performance.

- The criteria to judge the effectiveness of a coach are measurable improvements in performance on the "field of play." If the players aren't ultimately succeeding, it is preposterous for the coach to claim that they got the job done.

- Find out what the prospective coach thinks are the most significant barriers you have identified to achieving your Focused Intent. Given what is currently foreseeable, how might your coach reinforce your ability to succeed?

- Being a student open to the world around you is a path toward greater success and accelerated learning. Your affirmative attitude, your enthusiasm, and your openness to receive contributions from your environment are priceless assets.

- The moment commitments are generated, they begin to degrade and are subject to incomplete recall and distorted interpretation. I call this phenomenon the half-life of commitments.

- Your courage, with the aid of your coach, to reinforce the practical applications of your High-Performance Operating System underlies the character to win.

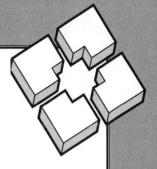

CHAPTER **11.0**

Hearts and Minds
Practicing, listening, and selling

"The greatest problem in communication is the illusion that it has been accomplished."

—GEORGE BERNARD SHAW, PLAYWRIGHT

 Preview

11.1 Practice your practice Phone calls, e-mails, meetings, and water-cooler chats—these commonplace activities are the playing field as you advance your goals.

11.2 Start, look, listen Observation in communication starts with intellectual honesty. The capacity to see and then tell the truth about what's actually happening in our private thoughts provides the material for constructive change.

11.3 Someone's sellin'; someone's buyin' You require a replicable process to quickly and gracefully stir others to intended action. Your ability to influence and direct others, by using practical, down-to-earth methods will flow from your High-Performance Operating System.

11.4 Win them over Mobilization is a frame of reference for building your relationships. The steps in this section will guide you to mobilize others successfully.

11.1 Practice your practice

You now have a Network of Assistance and a powerful set of tools to produce solutions that are in-line with your High-Performance Operating System. These tools, such as eliciting commitment and maintaining focus, are novel concepts and perspectives for accomplishing everyday challenges at work. Once you gain experience in applying and practicing the elements of your high-performance toolkit, your competence will evolve naturally. Using what you've learned in practical situations, such as talking to coworkers or planning project solutions, will foster your confidence and ramp your momentum toward accomplishments.

The various daily discussions and meetings that you manage or participate in are the interactive applications of your High-Performance Operating System. Phone calls, e-mails, presentations, and water-cooler chats—all these commonplace activities form the playing field as you advance your goals. You will achieve your Focused Intent one conversation at a time. Every contact has the potential to propel actions forward and generate results:

- As you maintain your attention with your intention, practical insights will follow.
- Each interaction can be purposeful without being rigid or closed to spontaneous invention.
- Every exchange can progress along a methodical yet unpretentious course of conversation that can be satisfying to your associates and to you.

The key to sustaining movement is to practice your skills and discover where and how your toolkit will enable you to gracefully accomplish your aims in new ways. The remainder of this section gives guidelines for using the tools and outlines five stages for structuring and managing meetings and structured conversations for conducting business, such as phone calls and one-on-one discussions:

A. Set a frame of reference or context.
B. Manage the meeting process.

C. Use the Problem Resolution Methodology.

D. Achieve *Net Results.*

E. Provide *closure.*

A. Set a frame of reference or context

The absence of a lucid frame of reference leads to fragmented discourse and tiresomely slow progress. To avoid or minimize such difficulties, follow these four steps in your preplanning and at the start of the meeting:

1. Establish start and end times for the meeting.
2. Assign a purpose for every discussion to make clear the intent of the meeting. For example:
   - "The purpose of this meeting is to track progress and resolve issues."
   - "Our intent today is to discuss our respective proposals and agree on a common path that we will take."
3. Determine the results you want to produce. Share them with others if they are common objectives. If you have personal objectives for the meeting, such as gaining support for an initiative, note them privately and keep track of your progress toward them.
4. Develop a logical framework for navigating the discussion. Establishing a pertinent context and an understandable outline for the meeting is very different from the disjointed "laundry list" of topics that people often assemble to discuss. For example:
   - Sales report
   - Fall campaign
   - HR issues
   - New-product problems

   What is the common objective of these topics? How are they connected within an overall framework of planning and accomplishment? (I provide constructive examples in the next section.)

B. Manage the meeting process

The following four steps are intended to guide your design and allow you to manage (and run) the meeting with more confidence.

1. <u>Share the meeting outline</u> with others and get their concurrence. You can often state agenda items as "what" or "how" questions in order to invite participation. As an example, I've organized the above "laundry list" of topics and have given a coherent purpose and stated the intended objectives as questions:
   - "The purpose of this meeting is to review our progress on our sales and marketing goals and to resolve any issues that are stopping us from moving ahead effectively."
   - "How do the current sales results track against our original monthly targets?"
   - "What are the most important elements of the fall campaign?"
   - "How can every employee contribute to our recruitment demands for new sales reps?"
   - "What new-product introduction problems can we anticipate and avoid in our marketing approach?"

2. <u>Start the meeting on time,</u> and end on time. Time is an arena of our lives over which we can begin to regain sovereignty. Managing time efficiently begins to demonstrate that realizing larger, more ambitious projects is credible. Arriving chronically late for meetings and appointments, or having discussions run interminably, disrespects others and undermines your trustworthiness.

> **"All that matters on the chessboard is good moves."**
> —BOBBY FISCHER, WORLD CHESS CHAMPION

3. Always be aware that <u>you are managing the dialogue.</u> If you are leading the discussion, step up to the opportunity with collaborative yet firm direction. If you are attending someone else's meeting as a participant, offer clear support

of the points to be covered and outline a workable process if the meeting trails off into the weeds.

4. <u>Keep moving toward your intention</u> in the conversation. Notice whenever the discussion moves off track or becomes bogged down. Gently bring the discussion back to the point or get it moving again. For example, you might say:
   - "How does your contribution connect to our current topic?"
   - "Can we make a note of that (see "parking lot," below) and cover it later?"
   - "Please hold that thought and we'll return to it."
   - "Does anyone have any ideas to move us forward?"

5. <u>Set up a "parking lot"</u> for random items that will be addressed at a later time.

C. Use the Problem Resolution Methodology

Identifying issues and potential problems early is essential. Within the framework of the meeting, ensure that the items for discussion, where appropriate, reach into solutions rather than just glancing over topics. Institute the practice of people contributing, rather than concealing, problems for resolution. You will set the tone for this style of communicating and managing with your Network of Assistance and your coach. Continue the practice in meetings you chair or attend.

When you are tackling issues or problems that require a concerted effort, use the Problem Resolution Methodology that we covered in Chapter 8.2. Applying the methodology will ensure you skillfully and constructively manage the interactions that take place in the meeting. For example, you can use the methodology to conduct a structured brainstorming session while you write people's detailed responses on a whiteboard.

The methodology can also allow for a less formal exchange, where you can quickly develop an effective action plan. In this case, participants experienced with the process, work through each step of the methodology in a fluid working conversation.

The activities of an emergency medical team vividly demonstrate the applied distinctions of the Problem Resolution Methodology. Using their professional competence, the team members would carry out the four steps of the methodology as follows:

- **Powerful question:** The context that guides the medical team is "What's the best way to get this patient to the proper care facility?" This unspoken inquiry underlies the work of the team as the members assess the situation and decide what action to undertake.
- **Current situation:** Team members do a quick but accurate reading of the facts: nature of the incident, age, gender, vital signs, prior history.
- **Proposals:** The medical emergency team quickly discusses and weighs possible plans of action. What is the best method of moving the patient safely? What medication or treatment can we administer immediately? What critical risk factors should we watch for?
- **Commitments to act:** Team members engage in a flurry of coordinated actions with certainty and a collective sensitivity to what else is happening around them. The team is operating on the field of its area of competence through taking committed actions.

These sample steps can be translated to the working collaboration of your team or board and their field of expertise. The steps of the Problem Resolution Methodology are not arbitrary but were gleaned from observing the core distinctions that occur in high-performance teams. These are the actions that appear "natural" and "effortless" when they come together productively in the service of an important challenge. Make these straightforward practices the heart of your high-performance team practices.

D. Achieve Net Results

In a meeting you're chairing, direct your remarks and the remarks of others to achieve a Net Result. This is the point of the discussion, the equivalent of scoring a goal in an athletic contest. *Display 11.1* will give you additional graphic direction to follow:

Imagine *Display 11.1* (following page) as a soccer field. A "field of play," if you will. The field of play has boundaries plus goalposts with a "net." The boundaries are similar to the guidelines for a discussion. In addition, like the goals of a soccer game, the purpose of any discussion is to achieve a stated objective, or net result. The arrows on the field indicate the direction a given remark takes the conversation. These remarks either move us toward the declared goal or in some other, possibly wayward, direction.

On the field of play, you will hear three categories of remarks:

A. Points of view: These include judgments, opinions, feelings, and random comments. For example:
   - "I think that"
   - "I feel"
   - "In my opinion"
   - "We shouldn't"
   - "I like/don't like"
   - "Another issue we have to address is"

B. Proposals: These remarks move the discussion toward its stated "goal." They are ideas for consideration that could be acted upon. As noted in the previous stage, stating proposals is the third step of the Problem Resolution Methodology.

C. Commitments to Act. These remarks produce the Net Result of the conversation (step 4 of the Problem Resolution Methodology). Commitments to Act conclude the discussion with actions that resolve the question at the center of the discussion. They are actions sourced in the commitments of the team.

The objective in achieving Net Results is to manage or participate in discussions that reach productive and satisfying conclusions. The key is to be aware of the impact of your remarks on the intended goal. Remarks, like points of view, thwart the intent by directing the focal

Display 11.1   The Goal of the Discussion: *Net results*

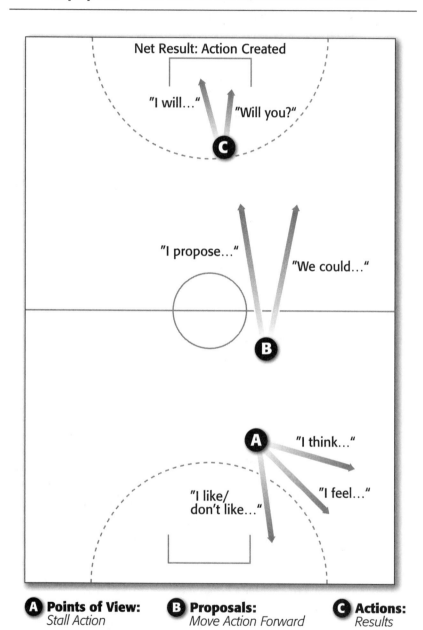

Net Result: Action Created

"I will…"   "Will you?"

C

"I propose…"   "We could…"

B

A   "I think…"

"I like/
don't like…"   "I feel…"

A Points of View:
Stall Action

B Proposals:
Move Action Forward

C Actions:
Results

point of the conversation "out of bounds." These statements, while they express feelings or strongly held beliefs, may prolong or confuse the resolution of what is being discussed.

Proposals move the focus of the discussion down the field toward a Net Result.

E. Provide closure

At every moment in a discussion, you have an opportunity to create something from what is being said. By tuning into the responses of the other people in the meeting, you can promote satisfying involvement and closure for the group. Build on the comments of others in ways that dignify their desire to contribute and move the meeting process forward. For example, you might say:

- "Jane's ideas provide a great platform for refining our plan."
- "Let's resolve Bill's concern. Do you have a proposal that would move us along, Bill?"
- "Can anyone suggest a way forward from what's being contributed by Claire?"

Giving others the experience that they've been heard will yield rewarding advances in the discussion. One way to accomplish this is to say back what you heard as they said it, word for word. Writing their contribution on a board is ideal. Nodding your head subtly also conveys comprehension and agreement. Simple yet reassuring.

At the conclusion of the meeting or discussion, acknowledge what's been created. Summarize and record the action points in an *action log*. The log is similar to others tools we've previously discussed to record commitments. Clarify the actions that were created in the meeting as commitments, with ownership and follow-up steps:

- Who?
- What action?
- By when?
- Specs for success?

State any expectations that weren't discussed or met. It is important to acknowledge what didn't happen and say how or when it will be addressed.

Thank the other people for what they contributed.

I will say more about the topic of closure in the next chapter.

Meetings are the playing field for your work. Practice the skill of conducting useful and engaging meetings. Your efforts will pay dividends in the results that you and other people produce and in others' enthusiasm to repeatedly provide what's required.

11.2   Start, look, listen

The stages we've covered strengthen your abilities to structure and manage conversations and meetings. You can gain mastery of these visible disciplines through diligent practice. The inner aptitudes of expanded observation, focused attention, and creative response are also learned skills. We gain access to these high-performance abilities through awareness, practice, and invention.

Observation in communication starts with intellectual honesty. The capacity to see and then tell the truth about what's actually happening in our private thoughts provides the material for constructive change. This change is desirable only if you recognize that the limitations of default attention wouldn't permit you to move past your historic thresholds of effectiveness.

One place to shift your default focus is your process for listening for and reaching agreement. This process also regulates your capacity to workably handle disagreement. *Display 11.2* illustrates our

> "I'm a real perfectionist. But that's the irony. In order to do it perfectly, I have to let go of perfection a little. For instance, in diving there's a 'sweet spot' on the board, right at the end. I can't always hit it perfectly. Sometimes, I'm a little back from it. Sometimes, I'm a little over. But the judges can't tell that. I have to deal with whatever takeoff I have been given. I can't leave my mind on the board. ... I have to stay in the present. I have to be relaxed enough to clue into the memory tape of how to do it. ... That's why I train so hard—not just to do it right, but to do it right from all the wrong places."
> —GREG LOUGANIS, OLYMPIC DIVER, GOLD MEDALIST

default and high-performance sequences of thought and evaluation of what others are saying.

Display 11.2   Clarity, Understanding, and Agreement

Default Operating System	High-Performance Operating System
1. Agree/disagree	1. Seek clarity
2. Seek corroboration	2. Reach understanding
3. Reinforce position	3. Agree/disagree

In the "Default" column, the sequence of thought is as follows:

1. **Agree/disagree.** We have an existing point of view, which we may or may not acknowledge. The point of view could be a belief based on prior experience or an unconscious process or emotion. It shapes the way we regard what is being presented. The awful truth is that the belief has us; it shapes and determines how we "think" and how we evaluate information.

   An example of a point of view would be our belief that advertising is inappropriate for law firms.

2. **Seek corroboration.** We select evidence in our environment to reinforce our already fixed view. The result is a self-limiting pull from impartial understanding and objectivity.

   For example, we are derisive of law firm advertisements and call them "sleazy" or "corny" or unethical.

3. **Reinforce our position.** We reinforce the clarity of our position for or against the issue through our self-serving default logic. We arrive at this affirmation by applying silent, unobserved force to our process of objective thinking. The force is required to hold our already determined position.

For example, after seeing the facts, we are certain that our decision regarding this matter of advertising for the law firm is final and correct.

Throughout this default sequence, we seldom open our critical facilities to think creatively about the merits of what others impart. In most cases, we arrive at the conclusion with which we started.

In the "High-Performance Operating System" column, the alternative sequence is as follows:

1. **Seek clarity.** We seek to first gain clarity about what's being presented. We achieve clarification by giving feedback to the speaker in the same terms and language they offered. The feedback sets up undistorted reception to what has been said. I call it establishing *dial tone*. Giving others the benefit of receiving what they said, as they said it, is not agreement. It simply communicates you are on the "same page" so the conversation can then proceed.

    To use the law firm example again, our feedback might be: "You want us to consider new marketing approaches for law firms to expand their client base. Is that correct?"

2. **Reach understanding.** After clarifying what has been initially said, the next step is to understand its meaning and implications. This includes other questions that come up during an open-minded inquiry.

    For example, we might say, "Does anyone have any ethical questions or concerns about client sensitivities to advertising in this manner?" This question is asked in a neutral manner and is not a statement of objection disguised as an open-minded question.

3. **Agree/disagree.** Once we've clarified what is being offered and fully understood its implications, we are now free to agree or disagree with the proposition. Our agreement or non-agreement is a commitment created as an informed and current choice.

To illustrate: "Having considered your proposal, I think the potential risks of advertising a law firm's services outweigh the immediate gains."

In this sequence, your conclusion results from clearly evaluating and connecting with what's been said. You've brought dignity to the conversation by demonstrating refined high-performance skills and extending respect that honors others in the discussion.

11.3 Someone's sellin'; someone's buyin'

All of us experience conversations that move us to think and act in new and exciting ways. Our view of ourselves and the choices that are open to us are altered in these memorable encounters. What conditions are present in these moments that produce inspired action? Is it just a matter of chemistry or unique timing? I suggest it has more to do with authentic dialogue and enthused motivation.

You require a replicable process to quickly and gracefully stir others to intended action. Aside from random chance, you will actualize your Focused Intent through your ability to influence and direct others, using practical, down-to-earth methods that flow from your High-Performance Operating System.

The inner aptitudes of expanded observation, focused attention, and creative response are also learned skills. We gain access to these High-Performance abilities through awareness, practice, and invention.

It is rare to find someone today who calls themselves a "salesperson." Most business cards for sales-related functions describe the bearer as "account executive," "company representative," "marketing consultant," or some other trendy euphemism. I suspect the reason for this creative titling is that people don't want to be associated with selling. It carries heavy default operating system baggage for many. In the default operating system, sales is defined and practiced as: "Getting someone to do what you want." I know there might be a howl of protest by sincere and ethical salespeople at hearing this description. However, people do associate selling with heavy-handed manipulation, relentless verbal riffs, and other undesirable behaviors.

I have the highest respect for the theory and practice of selling. Selling takes place in virtually every interaction. It can occur with the very human qualities of connectedness, interest, honesty, liveliness, and self-expression.

In every conversation, we either buy what they offer or we sell "I'm not interested" to them. We sell the waitress on providing prompt service at lunch (and she buys it or she doesn't), or she sells us on the proposition that she's too busy to be especially attentive (and we buy it or we don't). Someone's sellin'; someone's buyin'.

People associate selling with heavy-handed manipulation, relentless verbal riffs, and other undesirable behaviors.

You and I have alternatives to the gravitational pull of controlling, forceful selling. These options are crafted from the values of the High-Performance Operating System: inclusion, clarity, communication, relationship, inspiration, and choice. I call these options *mobilization*.

11.4 Win them over

Mobilization occurs when you interact with people and create the opportunity for them to act on their commitments. In mobilization, you design a conversations with others in which they are freed to act toward what they care about. Mobilization is a setting for building your relationship with others. It involves the following:

- Relating to others in terms of what they really care about
- Including others, not excluding them
- Doing something with or for someone, not to them
- Speaking straight to people
- Moving past the surface skepticism that people often express
- Opening up new opportunities for others
- Participating in the moment with others

In mobilization, you are responsible that your actions reflect your values. You express your enthusiasm naturally. In doing so, you put yourself on the line, which is the opposite of holding back. Although you may not always be comfortable, you will surely feel more alive.

Although mobilization can occur freely and spontaneously (watch the behavior of children when they fully express themselves), the following steps will guide you in intentionally and successfully mobilizing others:

1. **Make contact.** People vote early in the process, so making contact is vital to connecting with others. Smile. Present yourself openly. Check out your body language. Are your arms and legs crossed or uncrossed? Did I say smile? Take the initiative to offer your name.

   Example: "Good morning! I'm John Anderson. You must be Lucy Chambert."

2. **Get related.** Small talk is not needless talk. It establishes a common base of experience that is at the heart of mobilization. Speak about the weather or where you're visiting on vacation. Stay awake to the environment in which the conversation is happening; it contains information to which you can relate. Be interested in what others say, and validate their points of view. Put your attention on them, not on yourself.

   For example, you might say: "Those are lovely flowers in the garden. Did you plant them?"

3. **Move the conversation along.** Once you've connected, ask what the other person wants to accomplish in the conversation and state how you're in agreement to these aims. Agreeing on common outcomes establishes the background and shared expectations.

   Possible examples that would develop the conversation are:

   • "We're meeting today to discuss the upcoming charity luncheon."

> "If you're trying to persuade people to do something, or buy something, it seems to me you should use their language, the language in which they think."
> —DAVID OGILVY, ADVERTISING EXECUTIVE

- "What are you most interested in covering in the conversation?"
- "Great, I'm also interested in discussing the background on the anticipated guests."

4. **Build possibilities.** Now focus on creating ideas and possibilities that fit within the stated framework of expectations for the discussion. Clarify and build on what is being said in a process of relating and creating together. Seek to both understand and be understood. In the best cases, the conversation becomes animated and develops on itself. The ideas and possibilities are essentially proposals for what can happen.

    For instance:

    - "The theme for this year's luncheon could be 'Service to the Community.'"
    - "How do you see that theme being communicated to the members?"
    - "I like the idea of yellow and blue as the color scheme."
    - "We could bring in a jazz trio to play during cocktails."

5. **Make it happen.** In your discussion, you've raised some ideas and possibilities that require a bridge to the future. Summarize what you've heard and suggest some appropriate actions. When you've agreed on or amended each opportunity you've outlined, firm up the commitments to act. Here's what you'll do, and this is what they'll do. Secure the action in clear timeframes. Yes, it's all about commitment.

    You could say, for example:

    - "Let's review what we've established."
    - "Are you willing to be a sponsor for this year's event?"
    - "I'll make sure you're part of the welcoming committee."
    - "The total amount of your donation is due by April 15."

6. **Look for potential breakdowns.** This step can be a quick and graceful transition to closure, which follows. Review

any immediate concerns or likely problems arising from what you've agreed. Now is the time to say what could go wrong. Speak to those possible eventualities in a way that reinforces your accord and partnership.

Examples:

- "Before we go, I wanted to make sure you knew that our service requires a prepayment of $500."
- "If it rains, we'll hold the celebration indoors."
- "If we have trouble ordering special supplies, we'll use the stock on hand."

7. **Acknowledge what's been created.** State again what you've agreed. Thank the other person for their commitment and for the relationship. Appreciation brings closure, honors the other person, and sets up the cycle of connectedness for your next contact with them. The circle is complete.

An example acknowledgment is: "Thanks for agreeing to host the luncheon. I really appreciate your sponsorship and generosity. We'll see you in April at the affair."

Mobilization is the name of the game. Whatever game you think you're playing starts and ends with mobilization. It's time to enjoy the game and get good at playing.

We engage with the world, as we know it, in a conversation. Mobilization is the key to have that engagement be a product of our High-Performance Operating System. This conversation with the world takes place in three modes:

1. **Private and silent discussion we conduct in our "heads."** The evidence for this form of conversation is gleaned by carefully surveying our incessant stream of inner chatter. I have previously referred to this inner chatter, in Chapter 3.3, as "having thoughts." These thoughts are largely the output of our default operation system. In order for mobilization to occur, we must override our reflexive routines. Creative

> **"The most important thing in communication is to hear what isn't being said."**
> —PETER F. DRUCKER, MANAGEMENT CONSULTANT

thinking, a function of our High-Performance Operating System, occurs in octaves above the reactive "white noise" of "having thoughts." Mobilization originates in an intentional course of action.

2. **Public discourse.** This mode comprises the everyday "out loud" exchanges: meetings, phone calls, written memos and e-mails, and one-on-one chats with friends and family. The primary medium where we perform and are able to mobilize others, public discourse is also where people in our life form views on who we are.

3. **Collective channels of communication.** Public relations. Advertising. Brand development. Corporate reputation. These communal images are designed as larger-than-life conversations. These collective channels influence and work through the other two modes of mobilization described above.

In realizing successful mobilization strategies, consider all three modes of communication. Your first challenge is to identify your inner chatter, where you are "coming from" in your communication with others. Mobilization is a process of self-discovery. It includes determining what you're going to be about. What are you going to create? Mobilization is not a place to get to; it is where you originate. It's an authentic expression of yourself and your relationship to others.

You now have the tools to design mobilization from your High-Performance Operating System. So whom must you mobilize in order to fulfill your Focused Intent? What do they most care about? What would enlist them to act in support of your Focused Intent? What benefits could you communicate that fit their world of concerns? Presenting your Focused Intent requires you to deliver your communication in multiple ways to reach the unique criteria that would mobilize each person. *Spec Sheet 11.3* will help you tailor your communication for your audience, whether one person or a group.

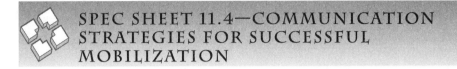

SPEC SHEET 11.4—COMMUNICATION STRATEGIES FOR SUCCESSFUL MOBILIZATION

Outline what you would say to mobilize others in your Focused Intent projects. These may be board members, teammates, customers, clients, your Network of Assistance, or family. (Example responses are provided.)

Individual/audience	What they care about	Benefits to communicate
(John—boss)	*(Revenue growth)*	*(My plan will impact growth)*
(Linda—assistant)	*(Inclusion)*	*(Her important role)*
(Client X)	*(Good service)*	*(New plan will add services)*
_____	_____	_____
_____	_____	_____
_____	_____	_____
_____	_____	_____
_____	_____	_____
_____	_____	_____
_____	_____	_____
_____	_____	_____
_____	_____	_____
_____	_____	_____
_____	_____	_____
_____	_____	_____

High-Performance Operating System—Cornerstone 4

High performance occurs in a medium of communication and relationship.

The previous three cornerstones—creating with others, envisioning commitments, and systematically solving problems—occur in a medium of communication and relationship. These seminal principles of high performance depend on a foundation and sustained environment of communication. Communication is the carrier for shared connection and results. Relationship is the experience of people feeling connected and aligned toward a common purpose. In every phase of your new High-Performance Operating System, the instruction of the day is communicate and build relationships.

In the final chapter of *Choose What Works,* I cover the completion of cycles of relationship that satisfy our sense of closure and restore us for new beginnings.

STORE IN MEMORY

- The various daily discussions and meetings that you manage or participate in are the interactive applications of your High-Performance Operating System. You will achieve your Focused Intent one conversation at a time.

- As you maintain your attention with your intention, practical insights will follow. Each interaction can be purposeful without being rigid or closed to spontaneous invention.

- Establishing a pertinent context and an understandable outline for the meeting is very different from the disjointed "laundry list" of topics that people often assemble to discuss.

- Identifying issues and potential problems early is essential. Institute the practice of people contributing, rather than concealing, problems for resolution

- Meetings are the playing field for your work. Practice the skill of conducting useful and engaging meetings.

- Observation in communication is desirable only if you recognize that the limitations of default attention wouldn't permit you to move past your historic thresholds of effectiveness.

- What conditions are present in those moments that produce inspired action? Is it just a matter of chemistry or unique timing? I suggest it has more to do with authentic dialogue and enthused motivation.

- Selling takes place in virtually every interaction. It can occur with the very human qualities of connectedness, interest, honesty, liveliness, and self-expression. In every conversation, we either buy into what they offer or we sell "I'm not interested" to them.

- Mobilization occurs when you interact with people and create the opportunity for them to act on their commitments. Mobilization is the name of the game. Whatever game you think you're playing starts and ends with mobilization. It's time to enjoy the game and get good at playing.

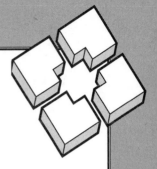

CHAPTER 12.0

Cycles
Ensuring closure, appreciation, and what's next

"There's a moment coming. It's not here yet. It's still on the way. It's in the future. It hasn't arrived. Here it comes. Here it is …! It's gone."

—GEORGE CARLIN, COMEDIAN

 Preview

12.1 **The sanity of closure** Closure is a method of communicating that brings order and meaning to a process, cycle of activity, or relationship. It is a way for you to recognize and express where you are so you can then move your commitments forward.

12.2 **All you need to know about "thank you"** Understanding and applying the principles of acknowledgment grows and maintains committed relationships and the success that flows from these associations.

12.3 **What you came for** Your ability to clearly and cogently state to others what you've gained will make your progress real to yourself, as well as your audience.

12.4 **Re-*Specs*** Review where you currently are with regard to what you envisioned when you first began the book and wrote your expectations.

12.5 **Your next *release*** Achieving your Focused Intent and assembling your High-Performance Operating System are designed as work in progress. This progression requires continuity, refinement, and innovation.

12.1 The sanity of closure

Closure is a method of communicating that brings order and meaning to a process, cycle of activity, or relationship. It is a way for you to recognize and express where you are so you can then move your commitments forward. An essential routine, closure corrects situations where we start boldly, wander though the convolutions of circumstance, and then allow matters to trail off into uncharted oblivion. Closure is required where things change, and those changes are not acknowledged or discussed. It is not necessarily a destination, or the final point, as commonly characterized. Rather, reaching closure is an entry point to a new cycle. Countless examples fit this pattern:

- Plans
- Resolutions
- Initiatives
- Projects
- Relationships
- Partnerships
- Personal feelings

Rarely do these kinds of relational structures of have vivid boundaries that give definition and a sense of fulfillment. In the absence of that clarity, you deny yourself the satisfaction and renewal of closure.

Lack of closure is the source of untold frustration, distraction, and bound-up self-expression. What you aren't saying, or encouraging others to say, presents a clear and present danger to the fulfillment of your Focused Intent.

Without closure, you endure or tolerate the clutter of countless unsorted conversations and activities that fill up your *storage system*. Against this background swirl of unstated change, you experience the anxiety of being trapped on an endless activity wheel. Worse still, the drain of these incomplete activities, relationships, and communications consumes your valuable capacity for creative thought and new direction.

Your default operating system mismanages (lack of) closure through elaborate mechanisms of rationalization, denial, and self-justification.

As a communication device flowing from our High-Performance Operating System, closure provides dependable supervision of these conditions.

You can provide closure within each of the endeavors in a number of ways. For example:

- Starting in a timely and orderly fashion
- Setting milestones
- Recognizing changes, modifications, and problems
- Insisting on open and complete communication
- Reviewing status regularly and fully
- Recognizing an end point

As I mentioned earlier, reaching closure is distinct from being finished, which is the acknowledgment that something—a task, a project, or relationship—has ended. The normal sequence of activity is <u>start, do, and finish</u>. Being finished is the structural end point, denoting the final element has occurred. For example:

- "My last day with that client was Friday."
- "The painter's work is done and paid for."
- "We mutually decided to end our partnership."

In contrast, reaching closure results in greater satisfaction and vitality. To reach closure is to say everything relevant about a situation <u>and</u> be heard. You and others are left without confusion, resistance, or argument. You can then move forward with clear understanding and renewed energy. The sequence here is more like <u>stop, make changes, and restart</u>.

Issues and communications that have been brought to closure cease to persist as problems or concerns that sap your energy. Some examples demonstrate closure:

- "Let's clarify the status of the project activities before the long holiday weekend. That way, we'll be free to take a break without worrying about what has or hasn't been completed."

- "I've done eight of the ten tasks I had scheduled for today. I can see now that I'm actually not committed to completing these last two activities, as they've reappeared on my to-do list every day for the past week. Let's figure out who else can do them if they still seem necessary."
- "We've reached a point where our planned work together requires a decision about going forward. We've not been communicating regularly, and the client's commented on our lack of coordination."

What you aren't saying, or encouraging others to say, presents a clear and present danger to the fulfillment of your Focused Intent.

Closure leads to sanity. It returns you and your relationships to now. You can then move forward without the encumbrance of the past.

Regularly bring issues and relationships to a state of closure. You will know what requires closure by your recurring thoughts about a task, project, or relationship. Pay attention to the silences and gaps in your conversations; this is where fleeting indications surface. Incomplete issues will jump into your thoughts and keep returning as *pop-up windows* on the screen of your mind. These persistent messages are the prompts from your High-Performance Operating System to reach closure.

Reaching closure is a vital practice of communication that has both utility and heart. Your courage in initiating closure provides a special advantage in managing and fulfilling what you and others intend to achieve. What you aren't saying, or encouraging others to say, presents a clear and present danger to the fulfillment of your Focused Intent. You and those you depend on for success are big enough people to talk straight about those matters that currently go unsaid. Clearing these issues will boost morale and performance.

"We hurt ourselves not by what we ask for, but by what we settle for."
—ALAN COHEN, AUTHOR

Spec Sheet 12.1 will help you to clear any outstanding or unspoken issues that may be hampering your progress with your current projects. Once you have written your responses, you can determine the most appropriate way to communicate and reach closure in the relationships that you have reviewed.

SPEC SHEET 12.1—REACHING CLOSURE

Respond to the following statements for each of the most important (or diffi-cult) people on your Strategic Board, team, and in your Network of Assistance. (Example responses are provided.)

Person(s): *John (boss)*_____

1. My concern about this person's performance:

*(He lacks patience, and he is not always supportive)*_____

_____

2. Comments I make to others about this person that I do not say to the person directly:

*(He undercuts my efforts sometimes)*_____

_____

3. Issues I have been unwilling to raise with this person directly:

*(His expectations of me)*_____

_____

4. My questions about the future of our relationship:

*(Can I ever please him?)*_____

_____

5. Ways I can support this person's success:

(Sit down and set/agree on clear objectives)

6. My current requests for support from this person:

(Please meet with me to review performance and expectations; give me a forum

to express my input to the way we work together)

12.2   All you need to know about "thank you"

Gratitude is your expression of appreciation for what other people have contributed to you. In saying "thank you," you create an environment in which your intended future can take seed and prosper. Your understanding and application of the principles of acknowledgment will grow and maintain committed relationships and the success that flows from these associations.

Acknowledgment goes far beyond the courtesy of thanking others for the obvious. It is a creative act that reflects your vision for the essential dignity and value of others. By creative, I am referring to your specific ability to recognize others in ways that illuminate their highest aspects. Such acts of generosity set the tone of your relationships with everyone with whom you come in contact.

I recall my experience on flights to Europe with British Airways, when I witnessed a simple but gracious act by the cabin crew. Each time members of the flight crew served a beverage to a passenger, in any class of service, they said "thank you" as they placed the glass on the tray table. The cabin crew regularly followed this procedure without fanfare or pretense.

In most cases, I'm sure the recipient didn't consciously notice what had taken place. But by their repeated actions, members of the cabin crew established a connection with the passengers while demonstrating their dedicated professionalism. Through these commonplace gestures a bond was coded in the relationship with passengers that effectively said, "Thank you for the opportunity for us to provide service to you." I am not surprised that British Airways refers to itself as "the world's favorite airline." They designed our experience and our relationship to them, in part, by mastering acknowledgment.

> **"The deepest principle in human nature is the craving to be appreciated."**
> —WILLIAM JAMES, PSYCHOLOGIST

To acknowledge is to recognize as valid. You bestow a gift on those whom you associate with and depend on when you can reach into their experience and appreciate how they see themselves. This skill, a mark of your High-Performance Operating System, is similar to citing achievement, which we covered in Chapter 2.4.

The domains of acknowledgment

You can choose to appreciate others in three domains:

- The realm of the physical, including objects and physical attributes.
  - In the realm of the physical, you might say:
    - "I love that outfit you're wearing. Is it new?"
    - "Your new car is really great."
    - "You look really healthy today. Have you been exercising?"
- The field of behavior, involving words and actions.
  - In the field of behavior, your acknowledgment might be:
    - "You did a great job getting the new proposal out."
    - "We appreciate you responsiveness in meeting our deadline."
    - "Your results are truly impressive."
- The sphere of character, comprising identity and selfhood.
  - In the sphere of character, you could appreciate people these ways:
    - "You are the most courageous person I know."

- "Thank you for your heart and your irrepressible nature."
- "I want you to know how much your partnership means to me."

Acknowledging others as you move through these domains, from the physical to character, becomes increasingly uncomfortable. You find it relatively easy to tell someone you like their jewelry. You are more at risk and exposed when you give heartfelt thanks to someone for the quality of their relationship with you. Aim to have your appreciation of others be fitting and a bridge to deeper levels of intimacy and connection.

Your recognition of others, thoughtfully weighted toward the "sphere of character," will more likely reach people in ways that matter. "I like your work" is an acceptable compliment. "Your work has inspired me to achieve much higher levels of professional success" reaches people on a whole different level. In this second example, you also reveal something about yourself: your appreciation, your aspiration, and your vulnerability. These attributes of your High-Performance Operating System have you be more accessible to others.

Position your relationships with people in the destinations of character and accomplishment that you all seek.

Remember, just as in speaking achievements (see Chapter 2.4), you are creating something when you express your gratitude. Look beyond the obvious and find what would validate others. Speak to whom other people aspire to be, not just their shadow. "I know you're capable of doing brilliant work. Would you consider revising this report to reflect more of the great concepts we spoke of?" Position your relationships with people in the destinations of character and accomplishment that you all seek.

I once volunteered as a kitchen assistant for an organization in which I was active. The chef asked me to go out and buy tomatoes for a holiday luncheon salad. It was winter, not tomato season. The chef, who had never previously met me, said: "Howard, I am sending you on an important assignment. I've prepared a special salad for the lunch today, and we require tomatoes to finish the dish. I know you are the guy to make this meal perfect. Find me 'great' tomatoes. Can you picture them? I trust your tomatoes will put the finishing touch on this special meal."

I searched four produce markets before I found what I considered were "great" tomatoes. When I returned with them, I displayed them to the chef and verified, "Here are the best tomatoes in the city!" I was so proud of my contribution. I never forgot the brilliance of this chef in viewing me as capable, committed, and worthy. With one phrase, "great tomatoes," and consummate skill in enabling others, he taught me a major life lesson.

Your default programming will drive you to see and comment on what's wrong. Obsessing on what doesn't meet our standards is easy. Instead, how can we speak to others, without being inauthentic, so that they are able to recognize and supply what's wanted? How can we motivate performance and loyalty in others while not overlooking inadequacies? The answers lie in the domains of acknowledgment.

For or not for

The subtext that underlies and precedes every one of your relationships can be reduced to a basic binary state. People experience you as either being *for* them or *not for* them. How others feel connected to you is never neutral. Either "I'm for you" or "I'm not for you" is communicated and/or interpreted in every interaction. When people feel you are for them, they will often boost their energy and output to remarkable levels. When they sense you're not for them, they will react with resistance, apathy, or overt solicitousness. Your genuine expressions of appreciation will shift how people relate to you, and they frequently become more willing to share and work in support of your intentions.

As well as acknowledging others, ask yourself if you are prepared to request what you would like to be recognized for in turn. You, and others, may protest: "I am self-motivated. I don't need credit." Such responses are reflexes from your default operating system. They are other ways of saying: "I can survive on my own resources. I refuse to be vulnerable."

"Be thankful for what you have; you'll end up having more. If you concentrate on what you don't have, you will never, ever have enough."

—OPRAH WINFREY, ENTERTAINER AND ENTREPRENEUR

In the default operating system, we relate to many commodities as scarce. When things are in short supply, we tend to store and protect them; we believe that if we distribute them, we will have less. However, appreciation, respect, and trust seem to conform to a different law, that of "the more you give, the more you have."

Praise others who have achieved what you are striving for. Recognize what they must be doing right to succeed. It isn't just luck. Appreciate the talent of those you regard as your competitors. It is detrimental not to see and build on what works. Your generosity in honoring others qualifies you as a big person who is capable of achieving and sustaining success.

Acknowledgment is not about gratuitous credit or feeding our insatiable hunger for "looking good." True appreciation speaks to and touches our deep commitment to contribute and to have our lives matter. You, and others, will continue to give your all when that contribution comes back to you as making a difference.

Spec Sheet 12.2 gives you an opportunity to design acknowledgement, gratitude, and thankfulness in your relationships.

Once you have determined the acknowledgments that you most want to give and receive, set up an appropriate time and location to communicate with each person on your list. First, tell the other person what you appreciate about them, and then raise any other undelivered communications or issues requiring closure. When this discussion is complete, say: "It is important to me to be know your view of me. How do you see me?"

When this person's communicated in response to what you asked, add, "Thanks for your candor, acknowledgment, and for our relationship."

Write down what you can recognize in others and in turn how you would like them to acknowledge you. (Example responses are provided.)

Person 1: *(John—boss)* _____

a. What recognition or acknowledgment could I express?

(He sets high standards that challenge me to do my best)

_____

_____

b. What recognition or acknowledgement would I like from this person?

(That I work diligently and often produce great results)

_____

_____

Person 2: _____

a. What recognition or acknowledgment could I express?

_____

_____

_____

b. What recognition or acknowledgment would I like from this person?

_____

_____

_____

Person 3: _____

a. What recognition or acknowledgment could I express?

_____

_____

_____

b. What recognition or acknowledgment would I like from this person?

_____

_____

_____

12.3 What you came for

You are now at a stage of development where you can acknowledge your progress toward realizing your Focused Intent.

You've used this book to guide you in building a detailed plan containing a comprehensive set of tools and perspectives to support you to think, work, and communicate from your High-Performance Operating System.

Those tools and perspectives include the following:

- An outlined set of expectations for the journey
- The foundation on which you're building expressed as "What's been achieved to date?"
- Your Focused Intent declared; saying what you will achieve and what it will impact
- A registry of issues and concerns developed, that detail what's most important for you to address
- Pathways for Action designed, which you and your Strategic Board will manage in order to reach your Focused Intent
- Major deliverables and dependencies clearly delineated, with initial tactics identified
- Key impediments outlined and moved forward, using the Problem Resolution Methodology
- Your Network of Assistance identified and enlisted to support your sustained efforts
- Coaching relationships established on a base of openness and receptivity
- Specific project management strategies drafted to handle your day-to-day activities and mobilize the actions of others
- Communication plans prepared to systematically allow you to build momentum, reach closure, and practice acknowledgment.

If you've simply read *Choose What Works* as a source of information, inspiration, and insight, I trust you've been served to this point.

Whether you've developed a complete blueprint for your accomplishments or simply raised your awareness of what's possible, we will bring together and consolidate your experience of engaging in this book as we conclude.

Your ability to clearly and cogently state to others what you've gained through working with the material in this book will make your progress real to yourself, as well as your audience. Communicating your Focused Intent is a leverage point to refine and assimilate your learning and your inspired actions.

"If I have been able to see further than others, it was because I stood on the shoulders of giants."
—SIR ISAAC NEWTON, PHYSICIST

For example, imagine you encounter a friend or colleague, and they ask, "What are you up to these days?" Or perhaps someone has seen you engrossed in reading and writing in this book and they say, "What's so interesting about that book?" You have just 60 seconds to respond in a way that is centered and compelling and that communicates your enthusiasm and excitement.

Your response requires a coherent statement of what you're up to and its relevance to the other person. Design your communication so the other person hears these seven elements:

- Your Focused Intent and your commitment to it
- The key deliverables and outcomes
- Some specific details of how you will accomplish your goals
- What's occurred so far, in terms of results or processes that are in place
- The implications of your achievement for your listener (remember the universal filter for listening: "how does what you're saying affect me?")
- Where you may be challenged or most at risk (this area offers the other person an opening to contribute to your endeavors)
- An invitation for the listener to become involved and support your efforts

After 60 seconds, when you have finished speaking, the other person should be likely to give the following kinds of responses:

- "How can I support what you're doing?"
- "I'd like to be involved."
- "What can I do?"

The following story demonstrates an effective presentation. The person delivering the presentation is a paralegal employed by a law firm. An associate lawyer approaches her and asks, "What have you been working on in that book you're reading?"

The paralegal replies: "I've been working on a plan to become an attorney. My intention is to receive my law degree in four years. My plan calls for me to be able to go to school in the evenings and still work here part-time in my current position. I'll also be supporting my young son.

"What I am really excited about is that I now see I can put all the elements in place to fulfill my dreams. Acceptance to school, a balance of work and study, arrangements to care for my son while I'm going to school, and the backing of the firm all along the process. My friends also pledged to support me in a host of ways once I told them what I was committed to achieve.

"I already filled out my application to law school, and Robert [a partner in the law firm] has said he can assist me in preferential acceptance. My folks will be lending a hand in caring for Dylan when I'm studying and at school. My biggest challenge will be to sustain the confidence and drive to succeed with my studies.

"My ultimate goal is to become an associate of this firm when I graduate. I was hoping you could provide some mentoring to me as I proceed through the process. Is that something I could count on? Is there anything else you think I should be attending to right now?"

Notice what works in the paralegal's presentation. She was able to cover all of the coaching points in a conversational yet focused and compelling manner.

Spec Sheet 12.3 is a guide to compose and refine your presentation of your Focused Intent and the actions you've developed.

Write a sentence or two for each of the points I've outlined, and then craft the sentences into a convincing statement that you can communicate in one minute. (Example responses are provided.)

Your Focused Intent and your commitment to it:

(I've been working on a plan to become an attorney. My intention is to receive my law degree in four years.)

_____

The key deliverables and outcomes are:

(My plan calls for me to be able to go to school in the evenings and still work here part-time in my current position. I'll also be supporting my young son.)

_____

Some specific details of how you will accomplish your goals:

(I now see I can put all the elements in place to fulfill my dreams. Acceptance to school, a balance of work and study, arrangements to care for my son while I'm going to school, and the backing of the firm all along the process.)

What's occurred so far, in terms of results or processes that are in place:

(My friends also pledged to support me in a host of ways once I told them what I was committed to achieve. I already filled out my application to law school, and Robert (a partner in the law firm) has said he can assist me in preferential acceptance. My folks will be lending a hand in caring for Dylan when I'm studying and at school.)

_____

_____

_____

The implications of your achievement for your listener (remember the universal filter for listening: "how does what you're saying affect me?"):

(My ultimate goal is to become an associate of this firm when I graduate.)

Where you may be challenged or most at risk (this area offers the other person an opening to contribute to your endeavors)

(My biggest challenge will be to sustain the confidence and drive to succeed with my studies.)

An invitation for the listener to become involved and support your efforts:

(I was hoping you could provide some mentoring to me as I proceed through the process. Is that something I could count on? Is there anything else you think I should be attending to right now?)

After composing a tight script, practice your presentation in front of a mirror at home. The tested method of preparation steels your delivery skills. As you practice, you will become more comfortable with the following points that comprise an appealing delivery:

- Maintaining contact
- Expressing enthusiasm
- Moving past the rough spots
- Communicating with power and grace

Your capability to articulate your aspirations, commitments, and plans is a test; your self-doubt is the examiner. Remember that you will be your toughest audience. Once you can say what you're about and where you're headed with confidence, authority, and ease, you will start to see that possibilities that you've created can indeed become real. Everyone else will follow your lead.

> "What we think, or what we know, or what we believe is, in the end, of little consequence. The only consequence is what we do."
>
> —JOHN RUSKIN, ART CRITIC

You will have the occasion to deliver your presentation in scores of ways to many people. When you have perfected the core message, you will feel relaxed in shaping it spontaneously to match the interests and concerns of your audience.

Your compelling presentation begins to reveal your growing competence with your High-Performance Operating System. Further mastery of its application embraces the following:

- Loving what you're doing
- Working like crazy to pursue your Focused Intent and your dreams
- Returning again and again to spend time on the basics we have covered
- Never giving your final attention on whether you succeed as much as on your intention to be successful.
- Recognizing the real opponent as yourself when you undermined by your default system operating.

12.4 Re-Specs

In Chapter 1, "Your Specs for Success," you responded to these questions (I have included them here for your quick review. Please refer to Chapter 1.2, "Your expectations," to reexamine your written answers):

After reading *Choose What Works*, I expect . . .

in my effectiveness at work, to be able to:

to produce results at work, such as: (name areas of desired results)

others will see me as:

in my satisfaction in my career to:

to be able to communicate effectively with: (name persons)

so they realize that:

in the area of my relationships, to feel:

to fulfill my dreams in new areas of life, such as:

Review your earlier responses from the following four perspectives:

1. Specific <u>results</u> that you and others have produced to date.
2. Plans, skills, and committed actions that are <u>in process</u> and will produce results.
3. <u>Your stand</u> for the future and the stand others have taken through your leadership.
4. This expectation is <u>no longer relevant,</u> or you don't plan to take action to realize it.

Put a number (1, 2, 3, 4) next to each response on the list of expectations. Your assignment these metrics will correspond to where you currently are with regard to what you expected when you first began the book and wrote your answers.

Now you've reached closure of this stage in your advance to fulfill your Focused Intent. You've done a great job. Congratulations.

12.5 Your next *release*

Achieving your Focused Intent and assembling your High-Performance Operating System are designed as work in progress. This progression requires continuity, refinement, and innovation.

I encourage you to stay with this course of action and build on what you've begun. I also urge you to review your plans, results, and achievements at the following intervals:

- In 30 days
- In 60 days
- In 90 days

Many of the ideas and practices for communicating and managing results will be deepened, and you will gain additional insight, when you return to sections of this book. In many cases, you can share the individual concepts and exercises that you gleaned from the book with others. Use your judgment to keep many of these ideas and points of learning in a comprehensible frame of reference. Take into account the context in which you grasped these views so that you can translate them to others with the full understanding, continuity, and perspective that I've conveyed throughout the text.

On completing *Choose What Works*, I advise you to ask yourself two practical and important questions:

- What did I get from reading and interacting with the material in the book?
- How and where can I apply what I've learned?

This book aims to give you a standpoint and structure as you take responsibility for your success and achievements. It also challenges you to see your relationship to your own limiting circumstances and to find ways to go beyond those barriers. Only then can you realize your real prospects for personal and professional accomplishment.

"Life is a sum of all your choices."
—ALBERT CAMUS , AUTHOR

When you can acknowledge your current limitations and reveal your courage in continually dissolving those boundaries, your enthusiasm for the future is inspiring. Everything you value will flow from demonstrating your character to succeed. In particular, you will naturally express the following qualities in your actions:

- An ability to communicate precisely, openly, and fully
- Skill and affection in relating with associates and friends
- Resilience in overcoming what life presents

Choose What Works is now the promise of your work and life. Please consider me your friend, partner, and willing coach.

STORE IN MEMORY

🔅 Closure is required where things change and those changes are not acknowledged or discussed. It is not necessarily a destination or the final point. Rather, reaching closure is an entry point to a new cycle.

🔅 To reach closure is to say everything relevant about a situation and be heard. You and others are left without confusion, resistance, or argument.

🔅 Acknowledgment goes far beyond the courtesy of thanking others for the obvious. It is a creative act that reflects your vision for the essential dignity and value of others.

🔅 The subtext that underlies and precedes every one of your relationships can be reduced to a basic binary state. People experience you as either being for them or not for them.

🔅 Your ability to clearly and cogently state to others what you've gained through working with the material in this book will make your progress real to yourself, as well as your audience.

🔅 Once you can say what you're about and where you're headed with confidence, authority, and ease, you will start to see that possibilities that you've created can indeed become real. Everyone else will follow your lead.

🔅 *Choose What Works* challenges you to see your relationship to your own limiting circumstances and to find ways to go beyond those barriers. Only then can you realize your real prospects for personal and professional accomplishment.

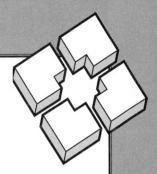

Afterword

I am most interested in discovering what you've accomplished after reading *Choose What Works* and the impact the book has had on your work and your life. Please inform me of your development and achievement by using the following *impact letter.*

Impact Letter

Write a letter to me, Howard Goldman, stating the value you have generated in your work, and in your life, since you read *Choose What Works* and developed your Focused Intent.

Construct your impact letter to reflect your situation before, and after, you read *Choose What Works.* Example:

- "My situation before developing by Focused Intent was …"
- "The actions I took were …"
- "The results and achievements have been …"

Cite actions and processes that are happening that are producing, or will produce, the outcomes you intend. What problems have you resolved and overcome?

Wherever possible, include specific measurable results.

Improved communication, focus, teamwork, enthusiasm, and satisfaction are areas to be covered in terms of your achievement.

What is your sense of yourself now and your stand for the future?

Please have your letter be concise.

Send your letter via e-mail to *howard@choosewhatworks.com* or regular post to the address below.

Your progress with the work you've begun will be amplified if the people around you and those supporting you are working with the same foundation of ideas and perspectives.

Share *Choose What Works* with your colleagues and friends. The processes and exercises are well suited for group discussion. Discounted prices are available for orders of 12 or more copies at *www.choosewhatworks.com.*

I and my associates are available to respond to requests for consulting and performance coaching for companies and organizations. Additionally, if you are interested in being trained as a consultant and coach to deliver *Choose What Works* to individuals, or as a group process, please contact us at:

Howard Goldman
howard@massociate.com

Management Associates
770 Crestview Drive
San Carlos, CA 94070
(650) 637-0404

APPENDIX 1.0

Plan on a Page

- Your statement of Focused Intent as the central navigation point of your vision:

_____
_____
_____
_____

- Your register of issues and concerns to be accounted for and resolved in subsequent planning and action:

_____
_____
_____
_____
_____
_____

- Your Pathways for Action to guide high-level approaches to achieving your focused intent
  (A)_____
  (B)_____
  (C)_____
  (D)_____
  (E)_____
  (F)_____

■ Assigned and agreed accountability and declared responsibility by your Strategic Board:

Person	**Specific Accountabilities**	**Shared Responsibilities**
_____	_____	_____
_____	_____	_____
_____	_____	_____
_____	_____	_____

■ Specific outcomes and time frames by when key deliverables will be complete:

Who	**What**	**By When**
_____	_____	_____
_____	_____	_____
_____	_____	_____
_____	_____	_____

■ Identification of interdependencies that are required to support delivery of results:

_____

_____

_____

_____

■ Commitments to Act that originate as coordinated efforts to remove impediments to success:

_____

_____

_____

_____

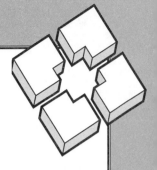

APPENDIX 2.0

Human Operating Systems

	Default Operating System	**High-Performance Operating System™**
Source:	Fear; something's wrong	Intention; something's possible
Trigger:	Need to "survive"	Conscious choice
Output:	Incremental results	Breakthroughs; innovation
Worldview:	Circumstantially imposed	Self-generated
Focus:	Activity	Outcomes; values
Motivation:	To have	To build
Identity:	Victim	Responsible
Payoff:	Being "right"	Being effective
Language:	Descriptive	Inventive
Method:	Routine	Creative
Strength:	Stability	Intentional change
Culture:	Unexpressed dependencies	Shared commitments
At risk:	Business as usual	Big rewards and failures
Mood:	Insecurity	Aliveness
Specs:	Historic scripts	Conscious design

	Default Operating System	High-Performance Operating System™
Time frame:	Present subsumed in past	Future initiated in present
Planning:	Reactive tactics	Outcomes shape strategy/action
Perspective:	Self-serving	Inclusive network
Relationships:	Controlling	Aligned interests
Communication:	Unconscious, imprecise	Clear, structured
Bond to others:	Expectations	Agreements
Status:	Through hierarchy	By making a difference
Learning code:	Hide mistakes	Contribute what works/ what doesn't
Leadership:	Forceful	Inspirational

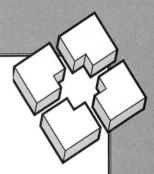

Glossary
Terms of reference

Achievement What you say happened that makes a difference. An achievement springs from an alternative, creative worldview that maintains that speaking causes something new to be seen. It's characterized as something valued, purposely subjective in its expression, and although occurring in the past, affects the way we regard the future.

Action Log The recorded commitments that are made in a meeting. The purpose of the action log is to display, review, and bring closure to these actions subsequent to the meeting. The log records who's accountable, what's to be delivered, and by when it's promised.

"And" A grammatical connection that is additive and inclusive in terms of the phrases that proceed and follow its use. "I liked the movie, and it was too long."

Applications Practices and tasks that are enabled and coordinated by an *Operating System*.

Attention The act or state of applying observation or focus.

(The) Awful Truth An unspoken, private concern that is the source of collective tension in a relationship or group.

When expressed, the awful truth usually results in a relaxation of concern and an opening to discuss solutions and alternatives.

Bandwidth The capacity for data transfer of an electronic communications system; a range of energies over which a person(s) or (system) can operate.

Being Responsible The stand people take based on their willingness to see themselves in a new relationship to the circumstances of their life. Responsibility exists in relationship to those commitments a person declares, where the normal cycle of cause and effect is reexamined. Being responsible brings into practice a relationship to circumstances outside of fault, blame, guilt, or default reactions (see *Default Operating System*).

Blank disk A data storage device/media that has not received or is devoid of recorded information.

Breakthrough An opportunity to take action, especially in circumstances where one has been stalled or thwarted. Breakthroughs are a new avenue in researching a cure rather than the resultant cure.

"But" An interjection that negates the phrase or validity of information that precedes its use. "I liked the movie, but it was too long."

Choices Options selected from the distinctions (ideas) available to us.

Closure A method of communicating that brings order and meaning to a process, cycle of activity, or relationship. It is a way for you to recognize and express where you are so you can then move your commitments forward.

Coaching A relationship dedicated to agreed performance improvements.

Coaching Journal A record of one's coaching interactions and the actions that result from these meetings and subsequent application of what was realized in these sessions.

Code The instruction set for a given computer program or operating system; a system of principles or rules that govern personal or group behavior.

Context A "background" or frame of reference that provides meaning to an idea, person, or object in the foreground. (Compare: *subtext*)

Commitment An agreement or pledge to do something in the future.

Commitments The intentional actions that define an individual, team, or organization.

Circumstantially imposed problems Our experience when we are in a state of reaction to problems that interrupt the normal course of events. Our relationship to these problems is they "shouldn't be" (i.e., we sprain our ankle walking down the street). (Compare: *Self-generated contexts*)

Created World View A sense of reality that is a formed from possibilities we entertain.

Creative Thinking (see *Thinking*)

Creative (realm) The ability to generate new ideas. Creativity occurs in a discourse we conduct with others and in the interaction of our (own) ideas.

Current situation This is a step (#2) in the Problem Resolution Methodology that is designed to record facts, data, or direct experience as the basis for generating new proposals for resolving and issue in action.

Default memory Our stored experiences that generate fear-based reactions within the default operation system.

Default Operating System The mode of thought and behavior that we revert to when we are faced with survival-based reactions. Our default operating system was formed very early in life and becomes the operational norm in the absence of alternative choices that we can acquire and exercise. (Compare: *High-Performance Operating System*)

Descriptive Relating and speaking in a mode in which we view the world as something separate from us that is static, enduring, and "real." Our challenge in this descriptive world view is to report accurately on what's there. This descriptive domain is contrasted to the *creative* realm.

Dial tone A tone emitted by a telecommunication device indicating that that the system is active; the reciprocal connection between people communicating on a common *bandwidth*.

Discipline An act of will applied to one's practices to maintain a commitment.

Display Screen The visual medium where the output of an operating system or operational projects are available. The display screen of our thoughts is an internal process where "pictures" of our ongoing interpretation of life are reflected.

Effective A primary design output of the High-Performance Operating System. Effective is an outcome where your actions matched the intended result and produce satisfaction.

Execution The act or process of performing an intention.

Field of play The arena where actions occur; one's workplace or forum for putting ideas into action.

Field of possibility An opening in which new ideas, perspectives, and opportunities are present.

Fire Alarms! A consciously dramatic expression of a concern or problem that is designed to compel attention to the issue. "We have a clear and present danger!"

Focused Intent A statement of personal /shared ambition that defines a clear (measurable) outcome over a protracted period of time (6–24 months).

Goldman Question "Are you on track?" ("How do you know?"/"What's next?")

Good ideas Expressions of what we want or what we will do that are not grounded in a powerful intention or commitment to act. The typical "New Year's" resolution that quickly fads from reality.

Half-life of commitments The period in which newly formulated promises begin to be undermined by changes of mind/heart, geographical distance, and the passing of time.

Heads-up Displays A prominent graphic that simply and vividly presents the current situation against the background of targeted goals of a project, initiative, or business.

High-Performance Operating System An organized set of choices and commitments one makes to experience a qualitative alternative to "default" reactions and thoughts. A defining characteristic of the High-Performance Operating System is one's ability to envision a possibility and commit to its fulfillment before one necessarily has the experience, resources, or know-how to achieve it. (Compare: *Default Operating System*)

How The plan for executing actions to achieve an *outcome*. (Compare: *What*)

Input Information fed into a data processing system or computer; the act or process of putting in advice, comment, or opinion.

Inquiry A systematic investigative process to discover what is true. Initially, in an inquiry, having the right questions is more important than reaching quick answers.

Issues and Concerns The set of normal topics and matters that accompany any endeavor or organizational arrangement. *Issues and concerns* arise when we have an uncertain future or processes for achieving our objectives.

Intention Determination to act to produce an outcome.

Interdependencies Accountabilities that require an action or delivery of interim results by another in order to fulfill. Dependencies require clear contracting of *requests* and *promises* to resolve satisfactorily.

Language A set of shared practices that convey meaning when communicated. Languages can be verbal, nonverbal, digital, musical, mathematical, etc.

Listening People's entire cognitive capacity from which interpretation and meaning is derived. *Listening* is distinct form the aural mechanics of "hearing." How we listen is a function of our biology, culture, experiences, commitments, concerns, practices. We speak based on our listening.

Logic A mathematical sequence programmed into a electronic device that determines the sequence of computation; human reasoning based on some rational design.

Mobilization The interaction that occurs between people that creates the opportunity for them to act on their commitments. In mobilization, one designs a conversation with another in which they are freed to act toward what they care about.

Mood The emotional environment that encompasses a person, group, or organization. Moods proceed what one thinks, how one "feels," and ultimately the range of action available to someone at a given moment.

Need-based coaching A default mode of coaching in which the performer "needs help" to improve performance. It assumes something is wrong rather than something is *possible*.

Net Results The specific *outcomes* intended in a discussion or meeting. Net results are obtained by managing these conversations so that *proposals* and *commitments* made by participants produce actions that satisfy the purpose of the meeting.

Network of Assistance The individuals you designate who can provide resource to your efforts to achieve a given *outcome*.

Normal Worldview A view of reality that is derived from given interpretations, experiences, and reactions. In this view of existence, the world is often a system separate for us and our interaction with it. (Compare: *Created World View*)

Offline An activity or conversation that takes place outside of the designated forum. "Let's take that conversation offline."

Operating practices The agreements and rules of engagement that are the basis for how a team or group will communicate, act, and behave. It is a social contact regulating professional conduct.

Operating system (computer) The main control program that schedules tasks, manages storage, and handles communication. Its core part is always present, and all applications must communicate with the operating system.

Outcomes An end state we determine as the measurable object of commitment and action.

Pathways for Action Specific segments of dedicated accountability, organized to structure and coordinate multiple initiatives toward a Focused Intent.

Personal Achievement Plan A concise design of objectives and actions that will produce one's Focused Intent. A "plan on a page."

Platform A computer architecture that uses a particular operating system; a declaration of the principles on which an individual or group stands.

Pop-up windows Messages that appear suddenly on a computer screen enclosed in relatively small boxes (often annoying when not expected); recurring thoughts that signal an area of our life that lacks *closure*.

Portal A door or opening for communication or activity.

Possibility An intentionally created interpretation of past, present, or future events, situations, and relationships. People move toward possibilities that reflect their interests, concerns, and commitments.

Powerful Questions Queries that we generate that provide a context for resolving an issue with the greatest opportunity. Powerful questions usually start with "What" or "How," as a device to invite open-ended thinking.

Priority Command The overriding logic of the default operating system. The default system will take precedent unless one makes a conscious choice to operate in a high-performance mode.

Problems Something that happens that interrupts a (background) commitment. Problems, while very relevant and real to the person experiencing them, are interpretations that occur in language. The person that has a flat tire in the opposite lane of traffic has a problem; we don't necessarily share this person's perspective or stress.

Project A detailed plan with a beginning, a middle, and an end. It is bound in time and can be readily tracked. You start by knowing where you are, and the project then progresses through specific stages (milestones) that build to the fulfillment of stated objectives.

Project management The rigorous planning, display, review, communication, and fulfillment of a *project.*

Promise A declaration that one will do something specific; take action to produce a result in an agreed timeframe.

Proposal An action in language that moves an idea forward toward resolution and commitment. Proposals are possibilities for others to consider.

Protocol A set of conventions governing the treatment and especially the formatting of data in an electronic communications system; a code prescribing strict adherence to correct behavior.

Reactive logic The reasoning/reaction that is produced in the fear-based programming of the default operating system.

Reactive thoughts A process of "having thoughts" that is a product of fear-based reactions. This reactive process is a function of one's default operating system. It is largely determined by events that occurred in the past that have command value over present circumstances. (See: *Thinking*)

Re-creation The process of energizing a commitment with its original intent.

Release An agreed milestone that serves to cause parallel actions and *projects* to converge on an important communicated event.

Request An action in language intended to evoke the commitment of another. "Will you?" "I ask that," and "I request" are all common forms of expressing a request.

Responsible A state of being where we experience our *stand* and potential for effectiveness. (Compare: *victim*; See: *Being Responsible*)

Result A "record of what happened." It is always measured and attempts to be an objective description. It is historic, in that a result happens in the past.

Results Management Structured processes to convert desire into intended outcomes.

(Being) Right An attitude or position we assume in which we are compelled to be right or seek to make another person or their point of view wrong. This is not a quest for accuracy; it is a defining reflex of our default operating system's drive to survive in all circumstances.

Scrutiny Rigorous examination of thought, practice, or planning.

See The cognitive ability that is made available to us by virtue of the distinctions we acquire. "Seeing" is a function of language; that is to say that ideas and words allow us to perceive what otherwise might not "occur" for us.

Self-generated contexts A senior frame of reference that we create to guide our experience and relation to potential problems. In this context, problems occur in relationship to our stated ambition. In that sense, we anticipate the possibility of such problems when committing to a stated challenge. (i.e., we sprain our ankle while training for the Olympics.) (Compare: *Circumstantially imposed problems*)

Source code The original digital script that was used to design a program or system.

Specifications for Success The conditions we outline that are the objectives for reaching satisfaction in a commitment or task.

Spec Sheets Specifications and conditions for performance of a system or entity.

Stand (Stand point) A declaration of commitment that defines your relationship to events or circumstances: past, present, or future. A stand defines the potential for reactions and actions one will experience and take. It is the basis for *being responsible*.

Storage The aspect of a computer system that files and retrieves data; human memory and recall.

Storage system (See *Storage*)

Story The reasons, explanations, and circumstances that justify why we produced or had the results with which we are left. These stories are almost always self-justifying. We are right; the circumstances or others are wrong. *Victims* inhabit stories.

Subtext An unexamined frame of reference in which we interpret current events and situations with an already formed, and usually limiting, point of view. Subtexts are a product of our default operating system. (Compare: *context.*)

Thinking A creative process in which we interact with present *inputs* in the most appropriate and effective means given our current, freely chosen *commitments*.

Time frames A specified period of time especially with respect to an action or *project.*

Transformation A dramatic change of perspective and identity that alters one's opportunities to take action toward an intention, without necessarily changing one's circumstances.

Utilities Programs or applications designed to perform or facilitate routine operations. (For example: How one deals with recurring doubts)

Victim A state of being where our commitment is to *be right* about why we are not *effective*. Being a victim doesn't require any level of *responsibility*. (Compare: *Effective*; See *Story*)

Visionary Someone who sees what's missing first and then acts to provide it.

Voting Exercising one's critical judgment and assessments.

What The specifications one creates for defining an *outcome*. (Compare: *How*)

Yeah, but The unconscious idiom (and *listening*) that limits the possibility of what's just been said and inserts one's *default* reaction. (Compare: *"And"*)

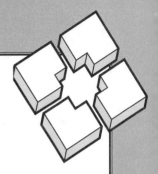

About the Author

Howard Goldman is partner/founder at Management Associates, an international consulting firm since 1978. They provide a broad range of services including the development of winning strategies, new ways of managing change, executive coaching, and the mobilization of high-performance teams.

His clients include: Apple Computer, Morgan Stanley, AOL Time Warner, Estee Lauder Inc., Land Rover, NEC, Computer Sciences Corp, hi-tech start-ups, Sprint PCS, and The Walt Disney Company.

Additionally he has served as a venture partner with iMinds Ventures in San Francisco, a leading early-stage investment firm, as a director of SoftBook Press, the pioneering e-book company, as well as director and strategic advisor to numerous start-up companies.

Goldman's career development includes serving as the Director of Artist Development for Capitol Records/EMI (working with such artists as the Beatles, Pink Floyd, and Linda Rondstadt). He was the chairman of the faculty of the Center for Management Design, a corporate university for senior executives. He lectures on consultative strategies at John F. Kennedy University.

He is recognized internationally as an innovator and expert in managing complex change initiatives that boost the performance, profitability, and satisfaction of his clients. He received the "Breakthrough Award" and "Leadership Award" from Transformational Technologies, his peers in the global consulting industry, in recognition for outstanding accomplishment.

He holds a B.S. in communications from Temple University. He served in the U.S. Coast Guard as a medical corpsman. He is married to Lisa Miller Goldman, resides in northern California, and has two adult children.